GOSPEL SHAPED

MERCY

Leader's Guide

GOSPEL SHAPED

MERCY

Stephen Um

THE GOSPEL
COALITION

thegoodbook
COMPANY

Gospel Shaped Mercy Leader's Guide
© The Gospel Coalition / The Good Book Company 2017

Published by:
The Good Book Company
Tel (US): 866 244 2165
Tel (UK): 0333 123 0880
Email (US): info@thegoodbook.com
Email (UK): info@thegoodbook.co.uk

Websites:
North America: www.thegoodbook.com
UK: www.thegoodbook.co.uk
Australia: www.thegoodbook.com.au
New Zealand: www.thegoodbook.co.nz

ISBN: 9781909919525 Printed in India

PRODUCTION TEAM:

AUTHOR:
Stephen Um

**SERIES EDITOR FOR
THE GOSPEL COALITION:**
Collin Hansen

**SERIES EDITOR FOR
THE GOOD BOOK COMPANY:**
Tim Thornborough

**MAIN TEACHING SESSION
DISCUSSIONS:** Alison Mitchell

DAILY DEVOTIONALS:
Tim Thornborough

BIBLE STUDIES:
Tim Thornborough

EDITORIAL ASSISTANTS:
Jeff Robinson (TGC),
Rachel Jones, Carl Laferton (TGBC)

VIDEO EDITOR:
Phil Grout

PROJECT ADMINISTRATOR:
Jackie Moralee

EXECUTIVE PRODUCER:
Brad Byrd

DESIGN:
André Parker

CONTENTS

 **PREFACE**

GROWING A GOSPEL SHAPED CHURCH

The Gospel Coalition is a group of pastors and churches in the Reformed heritage who delight in the truth and power of the gospel, and who want the gospel of Christ crucified and resurrected to lie at the center of all we cherish, preach and teach.

We want churches called into existence by the gospel to be shaped by the gospel in their everyday life.

Through our fellowship, conferences, and online and printed media, we have sought to encourage pastors and church leaders to calibrate their lives around what is of first importance—the gospel of Christ. In these resources, we want to provide those same pastors with the tools to excite and equip church members with this mindset.

In our foundation documents, we identified five areas that should mark the lives of believers in a local fellowship:

1. Empowered corporate worship
2. Evangelistic effectiveness
3. Counter-cultural community
4. The integration of faith and work
5. The doing of justice and mercy

We believe that a church utterly committed to winsome and theologically substantial expository preaching, and that lives out the gospel in these areas, will display its commitment to dynamic evangelism, apologetics, and church planting. These gospel-shaped churches will emphasize repentance, personal renewal, holiness, and the wonderful life of the church as the body of Christ. At the same time, there will be engagement with the social structures of ordinary people, and cultural engagement with art, business, scholarship and government. The church will be characterized by firm devotion to the truth on the one hand, and by transparent compassion on the other.

The Gospel Coalition believes in the priority of the local church, and that the local church is the best place to discuss these five ministry drivers and decide how to integrate them into life and mission. So, while being clear on the biblical principles, these resources give space to consider what a genuine expression of a gospel-shaped church looks like for you in the place where God has put you, and with the people he has gathered into fellowship with you.

Through formal teaching sessions, daily Bible devotionals, group Bible studies and the regular preaching ministry, it is our hope and prayer that congregations will grow into maturity, and so honor and glorify our great God and Savior.

Don Carson
President

Tim Keller
Vice President

INTRODUCTION

We live in a broken, fractured world that is hungry for the love and grace of Christ.

Many churches are committed to worship, evangelism and Bible ministry—but when it comes to getting involved in works of mercy and compassion, we're a little more hesitant. Will it somehow take us away from the Bible's call to make disciples?

But the gospel calls us to works of mercy and compassion. It's an integral part of our witness to the wider world.

The Christian gospel is wonderful good news for the poor, marginalized and oppressed: God has a plan to restore our troubled world into one of flourishing, beauty, justice and fullness. And the thrilling news for us is that Christ wants his church to be an active part of that plan too.

The Gospel Coalition has included this statement in their Theological Vision for Ministry, entitled, "The doing of justice and mercy." It begins:

> God created both soul and body, and the resurrection of Jesus shows that he is going to redeem both the spiritual and the material. Therefore God is concerned not only for the salvation of souls but also for the relief of poverty, hunger, and injustice.

And it concludes that, both as individual Christians and as whole churches, we have a divine calling to practically demonstrate God's love for the world:

> We must work for the eternal and common good and show our neighbors we love them sacrificially whether they believe as we do or not. Indifference to the poor and disadvantaged means there has not been a true grasp of our salvation by sheer grace.[1]

Historically, the Christian church has been in the forefront of showing concern for

---

[1] You can read the full text of the statement on page 158 of the Handbook

the poor and needy. From the earliest times, they cared for widows. They took in and cared for abandoned orphans. They founded hospitals and cared for the sick, they visited those in prison and they brought relief to the poor. And in more recent times, they have championed social reform to improve life in prisons, to end slavery and to bring in laws that outlaw the exploitation of the poor and helpless.

But more recently, there has been a growing suspicion among evangelical churches about the place of justice and mercy in their everyday congregational lives. They have seen that some churches, and even whole denominations, have eagerly embraced the call to do mercy, but seem to have lost their passion for sharing the gospel of forgiveness of sins through Jesus. They have concluded that this area of Christian life and witness is something to be wary of.

True, there are dangers. But, as we will see in this series, God's call to show his love, justice and mercy to our needy world is both clear and uncompromising.

You might be unsettled as you work through this material and see significant areas where you and your church are holding back from the clear commands of Scripture. Don't give up or try to avoid what the Lord needs to reveal within you and your church. Instead, prayerfully work through these sessions with the happy and humble confidence that God wants to use you in bringing the light of the gospel to our world.

Over the seven sessions of *Gospel Shaped Mercy*, we'll explore God's breathtaking vision for a world put right. And we'll get practical too, as we discuss how your church community can better show the justice, love and mercy of Christ to those around you.

Stephen Um

MAKING THE MOST OF

GOSPEL SHAPED

CHURCH

WHAT GOSPEL SHAPED CHURCH WILL DO FOR YOU

God is in the business of changing people and changing churches. He always does that through his gospel.

Through the gospel he changed us from his enemies to his friends, and through the gospel he brought us into a new family to care for each other and to do his will in the world. The gospel brings life and creates churches.

But the gospel of Jesus, God's Son, our Savior and Lord, isn't merely what begins our Christian life and forms new churches. It is the pattern, and provides the impetus, for all that follows. So Paul wrote to the Colossian church:

> Therefore, as you received Christ Jesus the Lord, so walk in him, rooted and built up in him and established in the faith, just as you were taught, abounding in thanksgiving (Colossians 2:6-7).

"As you received … so walk…" In other words, the secret of growing as a Christian is to continue to reflect upon and build your life on the gospel of the lordship of Jesus Christ. And the secret of growing as a church is to let the gospel inform and energize every single aspect of a church's life, both in what you do and how you do it, from your sermons to young mothers' groups; from your budget decisions and your pastoral care to your buildings maintenance and church bulletins.

Letting the gospel shape a church requires the whole church to be shaped by the gospel. To be, and become, gospel shaped is not a task merely for the senior pastor, or the staff team, or the board of elders. It is something that happens as every member considers the way in which the gospel should continue to shape their walk, and the life of their church.

That is the conviction that lies behind this series of five resources from The Gospel

Coalition. It will invite your church members to be part of the way in which you shape your church according to the unchanging gospel, in your particular culture and circumstances. It will excite and equip your whole church to be gospel shaped. It will envision you together, from senior church staff to your newest believer. It will enable you all to own the vision of a gospel-shaped church, striving to teach that gospel to one another and to reach your community with that gospel. As you continue to work out together the implications of the gospel that has saved us, you will be guided into Christian maturity in all areas of your lives, both personal and corporate.

This resource is for all kinds of churches: large and small; urban and rural; new plants and long-established congregations; all denominations and none. It is for any congregation that has been given life by the gospel and wants to put the gospel at the center of its life.

You can use the five tracks in any order you like—and you can use as many or as few of them as you wish. If you think your church is lacking in one particular area, it will always be helpful to focus on that for a season. But it is our hope that you will plan to run all five parts of the curriculum with your church—perhaps over a 3- or 4-year time frame. Some tracks may be more like revision and confirmation that you are working well in those areas. Others will open up new areas of service and change that you need to reflect upon. But together they will help you grow into an organic maturity as you reflect on the implications of the gospel in every area of life.

HOW TO MAKE THE MOST OF THIS CURRICULUM

Because the gospel, as it is articulated in the pages of the Bible, should be the foundation of everything we do, this resource is designed to work best if a congregation gives itself over to exploring the themes together as a whole. That means shaping the whole of church life for a season around the theme. The overall aim is to get the DNA of the gospel into the DNA of your church life, structures, practices and people.

So it is vitally important that you involve as many people in your congregation as possible in the process, so that there is a sense that this is a journey that the whole church has embarked upon together. The more you immerse yourselves in this material, the more you will get from it. But equally, all churches are different, and so this material is flexible enough to fit any and every church program and structure—see page 24 for more details.

Here are some other suggestions for how to make the most of this material.

PREPARE

Work through the material in outline with your leadership team and decide which elements best fit where. Will you use the sermon suggestions, or develop a series of your own? Will you teach through the main sessions in Sunday School, or in midweek groups? Will you use the teaching DVD, or give your own talks?

Think about some of the likely pressure points this discussion will create in your congregation. How will you handle in a constructive way any differences of opinion that come out of this? Decide together how you will handle feedback. There will be many opportunities for congregation members to express their ideas and thoughts, and as you invite them to think about your church's life, they will have many suggestions. It will be overwhelming to have everyone emailing or calling the Senior Pastor; but it will be very frustrating if church members feel they are not truly being listened to, and that nothing will really change. So organize a system of feedback from group-discussion leaders and Bible-study leaders; make clear which member of senior staff will collect that feedback; and schedule time as a staff team to listen to your members' thoughts, and pray about and consider them.

There is an online feedback form that could be distributed and used to round off the whole track with your congregation.

PROMOTE

Encourage your congregation to buy into the process by promoting it regularly and building anticipation. Show the trailer at all your church meetings and distribute your own customized version of the bulletin insert (download from www.gospelshapedchurch.org).

Embarking on this course together should be a big deal. Make sure your congregation knows what it might mean for them, and what an opportunity it represents in the life of your whole church; and make sure it sounds like an exciting adventure in faith.

Do involve the whole church. Younger children may not be able to grasp the implications of some things, but certainly those who teach and encourage children of 11 and upwards will be able to adapt the material and outlines here to something that is age appropriate.

PRAY

Pray as a leadership team that the Lord would lead you all into new, exciting ways of serving him.

Encourage the congregation to pray. There are plenty of prompts in the material for this to happen, but do pray at your regular meetings for the Lord's help and guidance as you study, think and discuss together. Building in regular prayer times will help your congregation move together as a fellowship. Prayer connects us to God, but it also connects us to each other, as we address our Father together. And our God "is able to do far more abundantly than all that we ask or think" (Ephesians 3:20) as his people ask him to enable them to grasp, and be shaped by, the love of Christ that is shown to us in his gospel.

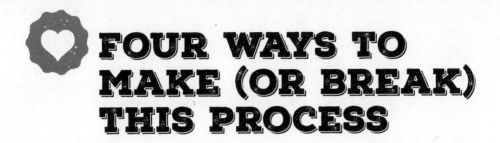

FOUR WAYS TO MAKE (OR BREAK) THIS PROCESS

1. BE OPEN TO CHANGE AS A CHURCH

As churches that love the gospel, we should always be reforming to live more and more in line with that gospel. Change isn't always easy, and is often sacrificial; but it is exciting, and part of the way in which we obey our Lord. Approach this exploration of *Gospel Shaped Mercy* by encouraging your church to be willing to change where needed.

2. BE OPEN TO CHANGE YOURSELF

This curriculum will lead every member to think hard about how the gospel should shape, and in some ways re-shape, your church. You are giving them permission to suggest making changes. As a leader, giving such permission is both exciting and intimidating. It will *make* your course if you enter it as a leadership excited to see how your church may change and how you may be challenged. It will *break* it if you approach it hoping or expecting that your members will simply agree in every way with what you have already decided.

3. DISCUSS GRACIOUSLY

Keep talking about grace and community. Church is about serving others and giving up "my" own wants, not about meeting "my" own social preferences and musical tastes. Encourage your membership to pursue discussions that are positive, open and non-judgmental, and to be able to disagree lovingly and consider others' feelings before their own, rather than seeking always to "win." Model gospel grace in the way you talk about the gospel of grace.

4. REMEMBER WHO IS IN CHARGE

Jesus Christ is Lord of your church—not the leadership, the elders or the membership. So this whole process needs to be bathed in a prayerful sense of commitment to follow him, and to depend on his strength and guidance for any change his Spirit is prompting. Keep reminding your church that this process is not about becoming the church they want, but the one your Lord wants.

HOW TO USE

GOSPEL SHAPED
MERCY

HOW TO USE GOSPEL SHAPED MERCY

Gospel Shaped Mercy is designed to be a flexible resource to fit a wide variety of church settings. The **Main Teaching Session** is the core of the curriculum—the other components grow out of this. The more elements you use, the greater the benefit will be to your church.

The elements of this course are:

- **MAIN TEACHING SESSION** with DVD or talk, and discussion (core)
- **PERSONAL DEVOTIONALS** (recommended)
- **GROUP BIBLE STUDY** (recommended)
- **PERSONAL JOURNAL** (optional)
- **SERMON SERIES** (suggested passages given)

Each church member will need a copy of the *Gospel Shaped Mercy Handbook*. This contains everything they need to take part in the course, including the discussion questions for the **Main Teaching Session**, **Personal Devotionals**, and the **Group Bible Study**. There's also space to make notes during the sermon, and a **Personal Journal** to keep a record of the things they have been learning.

Each person who will be leading a group discussion, either in the **Main Teaching Session** or the **Group Bible Study**, will need a copy of the *Gospel Shaped Mercy Leader's Guide*. This includes leader's notes to help them guide a small group through the discussion or Bible-study questions, and other resources to give more background and detail. In the Leader's Guide, all the instructions, questions, comments, prayer points etc. that also appear in the Handbook are in **bold text**.

Further copies of the *Handbook* and *Leader's Guide* are available from **WWW.GOSPELSHAPEDCHURCH.ORG/MERCY**

A FLEXIBLE CURRICULUM

Gospel Shaped Mercy is designed to be a flexible resource. You may be able to give your whole church over to working through it. If so, a typical week might look like this:

SUNDAY
- Adult Sunday school: **Main Teaching Session** using DVD or live talk (talk outline given in *Leader's Guide*)
- Morning service: **Sermon** based on main theme (suggested Bible passages given in the *Leader's Guide*)

MIDWEEK
- Small groups work through the **Group Bible Study**

CHURCH MEMBERS
- Use the **Personal Devotionals** from Monday to Saturday
- Use the **Personal Journal** to record their thoughts, questions and ideas about things they've been learning throughout the week

Or, if you choose to use the curriculum on a midweek basis, it may be like this:

MIDWEEK
- Small groups work through the **Main Teaching Session** using the DVD

CHURCH MEMBERS
- Use the **Personal Devotionals** from Monday to Saturday
- Use the **Personal Journal** to record their thoughts, questions and ideas about things they've been learning throughout the week

Or you can use the components in any other way that suits your church practice.

HOW TO USE EACH ELEMENT

These sample pages from the *Gospel Shaped Mercy Handbook* show the different elements of the curriculum.

All of the material in this curriculum quotes from and is based on the ESV Bible.

MAIN TEACHING SESSION

- 60 minutes
- Choose between DVD or live talk
- Discussion questions to help group members discuss the DVD/talk and apply it to their own lives and their church
- Guidance for answering the questions is given in the *Leader's Guide*
- Suggestions for praying together

This is the core of the curriculum. It can be run using the *Gospel Shaped Mercy DVD*, or by giving a live talk. A summary of the talk is included in the *Leader's Guide* (see page 34 for an example). A full editable script can also be downloaded from **www.gospelshapedchurch.org/mercy/talks**.

In each session, the DVD/talk is split into either two or three sections, each followed by some discussion questions. At the end of the session there are suggestions to help the group pray specifically for each other.

The discussion questions are designed to help church members unpack the teaching they have heard and apply it to their own lives and to the church as a whole. There are not necessarily right and wrong answers to some of the questions, as this will often depend on the context of your own church. Let group members discuss these openly, and apply them to their own situation.

Keep the discussion groups the same each week if possible, with the same leader (who will need a copy of this *Leader's Guide*) for each group, so that relationships are deepened and the discussions can build on those of previous sessions.

PERSONAL DEVOTIONALS

- Six devotionals with each session
- Designed to be started the day after the main teaching session
- Linked with the theme for each teaching session, but based on different Bible passages
- Help church members dig more deeply into the theme on a daily basis

Each session is followed by six personal devotionals that build on the main theme. They are ideal for church members to use between sessions. For example, if you have the main teaching session on a Sunday, church members can then use the devotionals from Monday to Saturday.

These short devotionals can be used in addition to any regular personal Bible study being done by church members. They would also form a useful introduction for anyone trying out personal Bible reading for the first time.

As well as being in the group member's **Handbook**, the personal devotionals are available for a small fee on the Explore Bible Devotional app. This can be downloaded from the iTunes App Store or Google Play (search for "Explore Bible Devotional"). Select "Gospel Shaped Mercy" from the app's download menu.

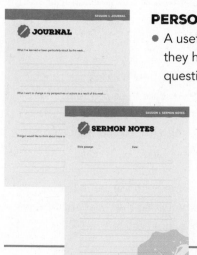

PERSONAL JOURNAL

- A useful place for church members to note down what they have been learning throughout the week, and any questions they may have

SERMON NOTES

- If the Sunday sermon series is running as part of **Gospel Shaped Mercy**, this is a helpful place to make notes

GROUP BIBLE STUDY

- 40 – 50 minutes
- An ideal way for small groups to build on what they have been learning in the main teaching
- Uses a different Bible passage from the DVD/talk
- Suggested answers to the questions are given in the *Leader's Guide*

This study is ideal for a home group or other group to work through together. It builds on the theme covered by the main teaching session, but is based on a different Bible passage. You can see the passages and themes listed in the grid on pages 28-29.

If possible, give 40 – 50 minutes for the Bible study. However, it can be covered in 30 minutes if necessary, and if you keep a close eye on time. If your church is not using the Bible studies as part of a regular group, they would also be suitable for individuals to do on their own or in a pair if they want to do some further study on the themes being looked at in the course.

SERMON SUGGESTIONS

The *Leader's Guide* gives a choice of three sermon suggestions to tie in with each session:

- A passage that is used in the main teaching session (DVD or live talk)
- The Bible reading that is being studied in the Group Bible Study that week
- A third passage that is not being used elsewhere, but that picks up on the same themes. This is the passage that is listed in the overview grid on pages 28-29.

FURTHER READING

At the end of each session in the *Leader's Guide* you will find a page of suggestions for further reading. This gives ideas for books, articles, blog posts, videos, etc. that relate to the session, together with some quotes that you might use in sermons, discussion groups and conversations. Some of these may be helpful in your preparation, as well as helping any group members who want to think more deeply about the topic they've been discussing.

CURRICULUM OUTLINE AT A GLANCE

SESSION	MAIN TEACHING (DVD/TALK)	PERSONAL DEVOTIONS	GROUP BIBLE STUDY	SERMON*
1 Shalom: The World Made Beautiful	God designed and desires *shalom*—wholeness, flourishing and fullness. Based on **Genesis 1 – 3** and **Romans 8:23**.	How sin has led to *shalom* breaking down in all areas: spiritually, relationally, in creation, in our institutions, and in ourselves personally. (Various passages)	A look at what *shalom* will look like in the future, and how this changes our present, from **Revelation 21:1-8** and **22:1-5**.	MARK 5:21-43
2 Justice: Wrongs Made Right	We do justice because God does justice. He wants his people to act on behalf of the oppressed and the outsiders. **Amos 5:21-24** and **Psalm 146:5-9**.	Snapshots of God's justice to train our hearts to love justice as our Father does. (Various passages)	A closer look at **Amos 5** shows that when God's people do not care for the needs of the poor and oppressed, this is false religion.	JOHN 8:1-11
3 Love: The Heart of Compassion	God calls his people to a life of love: self-sacrifice, empathy and compassion. We can't do this on our own; we need the Lord of love to transform us. Based on **1 John 3:11-24**.	What is love? A walk through Paul's famous description of love in **1 Corinthians 13**.	**1 John 4** shows us what the expression of genuine Christian love looks like.	DEUT 10:12-19
4 Mercy: Hearts Made Soft	Mercy is love in action on behalf of those in need, in response to our Shepherd's mercy to us. Based on **Matthew 25:31-46** and **2 Corinthians 8:9**.	A careful look at Jesus' parable of the Good Samaritan in **Luke 10:25-37**.	**Acts 6** shows us how the early church balanced the gospel call to provide for the needy with maintaining a focus on the work of gospel outreach.	MICAH 6:8

	SESSION	MAIN TEACHING (DVD/TALK)	PERSONAL DEVOTIONS	GROUP BIBLE STUDY	SERMON*
5	Generosity: Stewarding God's Money	What does the unjust use of money look like? How does the gospel enable generosity? Based on **James 2:1-10; 5:2-6**.	Key things Jesus said about money in six Gospel passages.	Checking our attitude toward giving against Paul's description of gospel generosity in **1 Corinthians 8:1-15**.	LUKE 12:16-21
6	Reconciliation: Relationships Healed	Reconciliation is something we receive from God, and something we must pursue urgently with others. Based on **Matthew 5:21-26** and **Colossians 1:19-20**.	Readings to help us see the challenge and opportunity of our calling to be peacemakers. (Various passages)	We see from **Philippians 4:2-7** how to help bring reconciliation to others in our church community and beyond.	MATTHEW 18:15
7	Diversity: Community Enriched	God's intention for eternity is to bring about beautiful unity-in-diversity through his Son. Based on **Luke 10:25-37** and **Revelation 7:9-17**.	Trace the story of unity and diversity through the Bible, starting in **Genesis 11** and ending in **Revelation 7**.	**Acts 11:1-26** shows us that struggling with racial division and suspicion in the church is nothing new, and encourages us to persevere in the pursuit of diversity.	MICAH 6:6-8

* **NOTE:** The *Leader's Guide* gives three sermon suggestions to tie in with each session. The first picks up a passage from the Main Teaching Session; the second uses the passage from the Group Bible Study; and the third is a new passage, linked with the theme but not used elsewhere in the session. This third passage is the one listed here.

DOWNLOADS

In addition to the material in this **Leader's Guide**, there are a number of extra downloadable resources and enhancements. You will find all of them listed under the Mercy track at **www.gospelshapedchurch.org** and on The Good Book Company's website: **www.thegoodbook.com/gsc**.

- **DIGITAL DOWNLOAD OF DVD MATERIAL.** If you have already bought a DVD as part of the **Leader's Kit**, you will have access to a single HD download of the material using the code on the download card. If you want to download additional digital copies, in SD or HD, these can be purchased from The Good Book Company website: **www.thegoodbook.com/gsc**.

- **DVD TRAILERS.** Trailers and promotional pieces for the series as a whole and for the individual tracks can be downloaded for free. Use these trailers to excite your church about being involved in **Gospel Shaped Church**.

- **TALK TRANSCRIPTS.** We're conscious that for some churches and situations, it may be better to deliver your own talk for the main session so that it can be tailored specifically to your people and context. You can download the talk transcript as both a PDF and as an editable Word document.

- **FEEDBACK FORMS.** Because **Gospel Shaped Church** is designed as a whole-church exploration, it's important that you think through carefully how you will handle suggestions and feedback. There's some guidance for that on pages 17-18. We've provided a downloadable feedback form that you can use as part of the way in which you end your time using the resource. Simply print it and distribute it to your church membership to gather their thoughts and ideas, and to get a sense of the issues you may want to focus on for the future. In addition, there are also fully editable versions of this feedback form so that you can create your own customized sheet that works effectively for the way in which you have used this material, and which suits your church membership. Alternatively, you could use the questions to create your own online feedback form with Google Forms or some other software, to make collecting and collating information easier.

- **RESOURCE LIST.** For each session in this *Leader's Guide* we have included a list of resources that will help you in your preparation for sermons, discussions, Bible studies and other conversations. On the *Gospel Shaped Church* website, you will find an up-to-date list of resources, plus a shorter downloadable list that you might consider giving to church members to supplement their own reading and thinking.

- **BULLETIN TEMPLATES.** Enclosed with the *Leader's Kit* is a sample of a bulletin-insert design to promote the Mercy track to your church. You can download a printable PDF of the design from the *Gospel Shaped Church* website to add your own details, and to print and distribute to your congregation.

- **OTHER PROMOTIONAL MATERIAL.** Editable powerpoint slides and other promotional material to use.

 WWW.GOSPELSHAPEDCHURCH.ORG/MERCY

 WWW.THEGOODBOOK.COM/GSC/MERCY

SESSION 1:

SHALOM: THE WORLD MADE BEAUTIFUL

AT THE BEGINNING OF THE BIBLE, WE GET A BREATHTAK-
ING VISION OF THE WAY THE WORLD IS MEANT TO BE. IT'S
A PLACE OF WHOLENESS, FLOURISHING AND FULLNESS - IN
OTHER WORDS, SHALOM. BUT AS WE LOOK AT THE WORLD
AROUND US TODAY, WE SEE BROKENNESS, HURT AND EX-
PLOITATION. WHY? AND WHAT IS GOD DOING ABOUT IT?
IN THIS SESSION WE'LL SEE WHAT GOD HAS DONE, AND IS
DOING, TO RESTORE SHALOM TO HIS CREATION.

TALK OUTLINE

1.1 • *Shalom* = peace. Both the absence of conflict and the presence of wholeness, flourishing and fullness. Shalom is shorthand for the way the world is meant to be.

1.2 • **THE BEGINNING AND THE BLUEPRINT** *Genesis 1:26-28*
Genesis 1 shows us God's blueprint for *shalom*. Three key things:
- Humans alone are **made in the image of God**—and have inherent dignity.
- Humans have been **given a job to do**—having dominion over creation as God's royal creation-caretakers.
- God makes men and women—he has created humanity for **community**.

• **THE BREAKDOWN** *Genesis 2 – 3*
Adam and Eve chose to disobey God. Sin vandalizes *shalom* and destroys it. We still see the effects around us:
- **Spiritual breakdown:** enmity between God and humanity because of sin.
- **Creational breakdown:** humans exploit creation.
- **Structural breakdown:** social structures (families, governments) are compromised.
- **Relational breakdown:** we exploit, harm, manipulate and idolize one another.
- **Individual breakdown:** we experience guilt, shame, fear, anxiety, etc.
Yet even in Genesis 3 we see a preview of the gospel—the promise of an offspring to destroy the serpent (3:15). Jesus died to make *shalom* (Colossians 1:20).

1.3 • **LIVING IN THE TENSION** *Romans 8:23*
- The Christian experience of *shalom* is held in an "already/not yet" tension. But Christ is coming back to fully and finally establish *shalom*.
- We've seen the beginning and the end of the story. While we live in the middle, Christians are called to pursue *shalom* in our communities, driven by the free gift of salvation in Jesus Christ. Works of mercy and compassion are an integral part of our witness to a hurting world.

You can download a full transcript of these talks at
WWW.GOSPELSHAPEDCHURCH.ORG/MERCY/TALKS

SHALOM: THE WORLD MADE BEAUTIFUL

* Ask the group members to turn to Session 1 on page 13 of the Handbook.

Discuss

What comes into your mind when you hear the word *shalom*?

This starter question is to introduce the idea of *shalom* and find out what people already understand, if anything, about it. Ask people to give just one-word answers—this will keep the discussion short.

▶ **WATCH DVD 1.1** (1 min 46 sec) **OR DELIVER TALK 1.1** (see page 34)

* Encourage the group to make notes as they watch the DVD or listen to the talk. There is space for notes on page 15 of the Handbook.

Discuss

"Shalom *is both the absence of conflict and the presence of wholeness."* Which part of this definition do you find most appealing, and why?

How people respond to this question may depend on their current circumstances. *Shalom* is a Hebrew word that is often translated in English as "peace." This is why we tend to think of *shalom* as meaning an absence of conflict, or reconciliation after hostility. These are both to be celebrated, and might be especially important to some group members.

However, the idea that *shalom* also includes the presence of wholeness may be new to your group. But it is a rich and exciting idea, so spend some time enjoying it and discussing what it might mean.

"Shalom *is shorthand for the way the world is meant to be."* Do you find this a helpful summary? Why / why not?

> In the talk, Stephen Um quotes this helpful definition from Cornelius Plantinga Jr.*: "*Shalom* is the webbing together of God, humans and all creation in justice, fulfillment, and delight." Seeking *shalom* is nothing less than trying to shape our lives, and the lives of others, to be the way God intended every part of his creation to be. (**Not the Way It's Supposed to Be: A Breviary of Sin*, p.10)

▶ **WATCH DVD 1.2** (10 min 40 sec) **OR DELIVER TALK 1.2** (see page 34)

> ✽ *Encourage the group to make notes as they watch the DVD or listen to the talk. There is space for notes on page 16 of the Handbook.*

 GENESIS 1:26-28

> **26 *Then God said, "Let us make man in our image, after our likeness. And let them have dominion over the fish of the sea and over the birds of the heavens and over the livestock and over all the earth and over every creeping thing that creeps on the earth." 27 So God created man in his own image, in the image of God he created him; male and female he created them. 28 And God blessed them. And God said to them, "Be fruitful and multiply and fill the earth and subdue it, and have dominion over the fish of the sea and over the birds of the heavens and over every living thing that moves on the earth."***

Discuss

"Humans are the only creatures created in the image of God. That means we have an inherent dignity that is different from everything else. This is the grounding principle for everything we are going to consider about social justice, mercy and compassion."

Why do you think our role as image-bearers is so important for how we think about social justice, mercy and compassion?

> All humans are created in God's image, which means that we reflect, in some way, his character. Look up the following verses to see how God himself views social justice, mercy and compassion.

- "The Rock, his work is perfect, for all his ways are justice. A God of faithfulness and without iniquity, just and upright is he." Deuteronomy 32:4
- "The LORD is good to all, and his mercy is over all that he has made." Psalm 145:9
- "As a father shows compassion to his children, so the LORD shows compassion to those who fear him." Psalm 103:13

This is the godly image that we are to reflect in our own lives. And as Christians show these characteristics to others, we are giving them a glimpse of what God is like.

But all humans are created in God's image, not just Christians. So our view of social justice, mercy and compassion should also be shaped by the fact that the homeless man in the street, the migrant trying to reach a new country, and the hungry woman waiting in line at the food kitchen are all God's image-bearers as well.

As God's image-bearers, Adam and Eve were meant to be royal caretakers of the world (Genesis 1:28). How did they fail at this task? (See Genesis 2:15-17 and 3:6.)

God put Adam and Eve in the Garden of Eden to "have dominion over" it (Genesis 1:28) and to "work it and keep it" (Genesis 2:15). But instead of caring for all the created things in the garden, and ruling over them, Adam and Eve allowed one of the creatures in the garden to rule them. They listened to the serpent, and disobeyed the Lord. This broke the perfect *shalom* in the garden.

Jesus was the Royal Caretaker of the world. How did he succeed at this task? (See Genesis 3:15 and Colossians 1:19-20.)

Ask the group for examples of how Jesus perfectly bore God's image, how he brought *shalom* to those around him, and how he made it possible for *shalom* with God to be perfectly restored.

- Jesus did what Adam failed to do. He perfectly bore the image of God, and he refused to give in to the temptations of Satan (Matthew 4:1-11).
- Jesus lived in harmonious, shalom-shaped community with those around him, particularly with those who were poor, sick, marginalized and ostracized (for example, Luke 15:1-2; Matthew 5:43-44; 9:10-13; John 4:7-10).

- We see the very first preview of Jesus restoring *shalom* in Genesis 3:15, where God warns the serpent that one of the offspring of Eve will "bruise" his head. The Hebrew word translated as "bruise" can also mean "crush," and Jesus did indeed crush the devil through his death on the cross. In doing so he was "making peace (*shalom*) by the blood of his cross" (Colossians 1:20). Adam's sin had destroyed the *shalom* of the garden. Jesus' death and resurrection restored *shalom* with God for all who trust in Christ.

"Sin vandalizes shalom and destroys it." Can you think of some examples of this in your home, your neighborhood, and your country?

The aim of this question is to help group members to apply what they've been thinking about to their own situations.

▶ **WATCH DVD 1.3** (5 min 0 sec) **OR DELIVER TALK 1.3** (see page 34)

- *Encourage the group to make notes as they watch the DVD or listen to the talk. There is space for notes on page 18 of the Handbook.*

Discuss

"The Christian experience of shalom is held in an 'already/not yet' tension." Complete the table below to see some examples of this.

ALREADY	NOT YET
Jesus has already made peace by his blood	
Jesus has already defeated death by his own death and resurrection	
	Jesus is coming back to finally establish *shalom*
Christians are already adopted by God	
	In the new creation all things will be made new

Answers could include:

ALREADY	NOT YET
Jesus has already made peace by his blood	We have not yet experienced the fullness of that peace in our world
Jesus has already defeated death by his own death and resurrection	Our world has not yet experienced the final outworking of that victory—the end of death
We wait patiently for Jesus to return, knowing he has already done all that is needed to establish *shalom*	**Jesus is coming back to finally establish *shalom***
Christians are already adopted by God	We are not yet face to face with God, but we look forward to being with our Father in the new creation
Jesus has already done all that is needed to restore creation	**In the new creation, all things will be made new**

While we wait for Jesus to return, we live in a fallen world. We don't fully experience *shalom*. What difference does it make to our daily lives that we can be confident that one day we will experience full, lasting *shalom*?

- We know that any pain, disunity or hardship we suffer is only temporary.
- We are not crushed or despairing when we experience difficulties—we know they will not last.
- We are not surprised when hard things happen.
- We can ask God to give us the help we need to live for him in difficult times, knowing we have perfect *shalom* to look forward to in the new creation.

Pray

☞ **REVELATION 21:1-5**

> [1] Then I saw a new heaven and a new earth, for the first heaven and the first earth had passed away, and the sea was no more. [2] And I saw the holy city, new Jerusalem, coming down out of heaven from God, prepared as a bride adorned for her husband. [3] And I heard a loud voice from the throne saying, "Behold, the dwelling place of God is with man. He will dwell with them, and they will be his people, and God himself will be with them as their God. [4] He will wipe away every tear from their eyes, and death shall be no more, neither shall there be mourning, nor crying, nor pain anymore, for the former things have passed away." [5] And he who was seated on the throne said, "Behold, I am making all things new."

LOOK FORWARD to the coming of the new creation, when there will be no more death, mourning, crying or pain. Thank God that you have such perfect *shalom* to look forward to.

LOOK BACK to the death and resurrection of Jesus, which makes this perfect *shalom* possible. Thank God for sending his own Son, Jesus, to do this for us.

LOOK AROUND at your group, your church and your neighborhood. Ask God to help your church family to live in a way that honors him and brings *shalom* as far as you are able to.

DAILY BIBLE DEVOTIONALS

As you finish the session, point group members to the daily devotionals to do at home over the course of the next week. There are six of them, beginning on page 21, and followed by a page for journaling. This week the devotionals show how far we have fallen. Each reading focuses on a sphere of life where *shalom* has been lost, and on how it leaves us and the world hungry for Jesus and his gospel.

SERMONS

OPTION ONE: GENESIS 1 – 3

Stephen focuses on these chapters in his DVD presentation, and you could expand upon it in a longer sermon.

OPTION TWO: REVELATION 21:1-8; 22:1-5

This is the passage the Bible study is based on (see next page), which could also be expanded upon in a sermon.

OPTION THREE: MARK 5:21-43

This passage is not mentioned in this material, but picks up on several of the themes of this session, especially the following:

- We see *shalom* at the start and end of the Bible: in Eden and in the new creation—peace, wholeness and flourishing. Our hearts are hungry for it.
- But we see it somewhere else: in Jesus. He gives life to a dead girl and stops the crying, grief and pain. Wherever he walks, the green grass of Eden grows around him. Jesus is where our desires for peace find their fulfillment.

If one of your Sunday sermons is to be based on the theme of this session, church members will find a page to write notes on the sermon on page 31 of their Handbooks.

BIBLE STUDY

AIM: In the main teaching session this week, we surveyed the storyline of the Bible and saw how it related to the biblical idea of *shalom*—the fruitful, joyful, peace-filled flourishing of people in right relationship with God, the world and each other. We saw it under four different headings:

- *Creation:* In Genesis 1 – 2, we see the perfect Eden that God made.
- *Fall:* That perfect creation was spoiled—*shalom* was shattered—by the disobedience of Adam and Eve. Since then, our world has been subject to all manner of evils that creep in when *shalom* is lost: injustice, and a lack of love, mercy and forgiveness.
- *Redemption:* In Jesus, God has done everything to restore *shalom* to people through the death of his Son. Now the gospel message calls people back into a relationship with the living God.
- *Fulfillment:* The world is heading toward a new creation, when Eden will be restored (and surpassed!), and the *shalom* won by Jesus at the cross will be revealed.

This Bible study will go over some aspects of this ground again. Never assume that your group has got this. And even if this is basic, those who rejoice to belong to Jesus through the gospel will enjoy thinking and talking about how wonderful *shalom* is and will be.

Discuss

If you asked people in the street to describe the world they would love to live in, what kind of answers would they give? What does this show about people in general?

Much of what people dream of—no more suffering, sickness, poverty, hatred, injustice, inequality, death, etc—is a description of life in Eden, and will be part of God's promised new world. Most likely, however, people will omit God himself from their ideal world.

It shows that people of all kinds have an instinctive understanding of and contact point with what is in the Bible, and what is promised in the gospel. We are made in God's image, and we are made for *shalom*. But we recognize that there is a huge gap between where we are now, and where we would like to be.

READ REVELATION 21:1-8; 22:1-5

¹ Then I saw a new heaven and a new earth, for the first heaven and the first earth had passed away, and the sea was no more...

1. What surprises you about this new world (21:1-2)?

Answers may include the mention of no more sea (21:1), and of the city and the bride coming down out of heaven (21:2). This is vivid picture language. The sea is a source of threat, so a world without a sea is a world of safety and security. Jerusalem is God's city, and the bride is a picture of God's special relationship with his people. God promises that people will know him and live in his new world.

2. What will this new world be like? How is it like the picture of Eden in Genesis 2?

Encourage people to get their answers from the Bible passage by asking questions like, "Where do you get that from?" or "Which verse tells us that?"
- 21:4: There will be no more death, mourning, crying or pain.
- 22:2: The trees supply abundant fruit—there will be no hunger. We get a picture of a fruitful, rich, stimulating and peaceful environment, with many of the features of Eden.
- 21:8: It will be a place of justice. Evil will be excluded.
- It is a place of life and healing—the river of the water of life (22:1) and the tree of life (v 2) are there.
- There will no longer be any curse (v 3).
- God's throne will be there (v 3), his face will be seen (v 4) and he will give this new world light (v 5).
- People will serve God (v 3), be marked with God's name (v 4) and reign forever and ever (v 5).
- There is a wedding in both Genesis and Revelation: that of Adam and Eve, and that of Jesus and his people.

Why are these qualities of eternal life so attractive to us?

There will be no need of handkerchiefs, hospitals or hearses in the new creation—these are the things that signify all the hurt and pain of our world now. Of course, when we look to the world perfected, it will be without the things that spoil life now. This gives an added edge to life in the new creation over Eden—it feels all the better because of the sense of relief at the absence of so much that spoils our life in the world now.

3. Who is at the center of this new world?

"God himself will be with them and be their God" (22:3). But notice that this relationship is intimate and personal—not distant and formal. God himself lives with humanity (v 3) and wipes every tear from our eyes (v 4), as a parent might comfort a traumatized child.

4. In the death of Jesus, we have been shown justice, mercy, compassion and inclusion. Christians have always worked to model these qualities in their personal lives, in the lives of their churches, and in the wider world. Where have Christians gone wrong when thinking about working for these qualities in these three areas? How does Revelation help us with this issue?

- Many Christians have made the mistake of making our Christian response to the gospel an exclusively personal thing. It is personal, but it is also corporate. God is saving a new community, made up of redeemed individuals.
- Others have made the mistake of suggesting that our response to the gospel does not require personal holiness. While the righteousness that brings us into fellowship with God is entirely a gift from God, nonetheless, the warnings of 21:8 show that those who are truly redeemed will grow away from these things that are destined for fire.
- Some Christians feel that our sole job now is to preach the gospel—and not to work for justice in a world that is destined for hell. And yet personal holiness and the renewed life of the Christian community are inseparably linked with gospel witness in the Bible. In the Old Testament, life in Israel was meant to be so good that the nations would look at them and be jealous for what they had. In the New Testament, Christians are to be known for their love for others, marked by a neighborly willingness to care for the needy (e.g. The Good Samaritan), and to live such good lives among the pagans that they lead to evangelistic conversations (1 Peter 3:15-16).
- Other Christians have seen it as almost their sole job to work for justice and mercy in the world. The preaching of the gospel message gets watered down

and then lost. This passage at the end of the Bible shows us that justice will never be truly achieved until the new creation, and that inclusion in it depends on having our names "written in the Lamb's book of life" (21:27).

- Yet others think that this is something that we must strive for ourselves, without God. Many political movements started from within the Christian church, but lost not just the gospel but God completely from the picture. This passage at the very end of the Bible shows us that the new creation is something that can only be achieved by God, and only at the end of time—not before.

5. How will the sure promise of the new creation help us when:

- **we are tempted to give up our faith because of opposition?**
  - Heaven is a sure thing. It is a promise from God that is "trustworthy and true."
  - But he also says that the new creation is for those who conquer (21:7). We are called to faithful service and witness to the end.

- **we want to give up working for justice, inclusion and mercy in a world that is unfair?**
  - We should expect both opposition and persecution in a fallen world.
  - But there are ways we can fight this fight and win ground, even if only temporarily, in our family, neighborhood, nation and the world.
  - To do so is part of our witness to the transforming power of Christ in our lives, in our church, and in the world.

- **we are overwhelmed by the needs we see in our world?**
  - The poor will always be with us (Mark 14:7).
  - We cannot do everything; but we can all do something.
  - God sees the pain in our world far more clearly and deeply than we do. He will judge those who have caused it; and he will bless those who, through Christ, have done something to relieve it.

6. How can this understanding of where we have come from and where we are going to help us share the gospel with others?

Everyone instinctively wants what is on offer in the gospel. A desire for peace, plenty and perfect relationships lies deep in the heart of everyone you know and meet. Because of sin, they may be disappointed and ground down by the everyday reality of a fallen world. Or they may be falsely optimistic about what they can achieve through their own efforts—but they want the same thing. This is fertile shared ground for talking about what God has done in Christ, and how they can be part of a new community that will ultimately enjoy the blessings of the new creation.

Apply

FOR YOURSELF: Which aspect of our fallenness do you feel most keenly? Which aspect of the new creation are you most looking forward to? Do you think you are involved too much or too little in working in your family, neighborhood or world to pursue *shalom*?

FOR YOUR CHURCH: Do you think this area of our gospel response is too small or too great as a congregation? What are you hoping to get out of this series as you study, think, discuss and pray together?

Pray

FOR YOUR GROUP: Ask God to fill you with a sense of assurance and joy about his promise that all things will be made new in the new creation.

FOR YOUR CHURCH: Pray that, both as individuals and as a church, you would find ways to express the justice, mercy, inclusion and compassion you have experienced in the gospel, both to each other, and to the wider world.

FURTHER READING

*"*Re-weaving shalom means to sacrificially thread, lace, and press your time, goods, power, and resources into the lives and needs of others.*
Timothy Keller

The fall of man has created a perpetual crisis. It will last until sin has been put down and Christ reigns over a redeemed and restored world. Until that time the earth remains a disaster area and its inhabitants live in a state of extraordinary emergency. To me it has always been difficult to understand those evangelical Christians who insist upon living in the crisis as if no crisis existed.
A. W. Tozer

Christ is much more powerful to save than Adam was to destroy.
John Calvin

Books
- *What Is the Mission of the Church? Making Sense of Social Justice, Shalom, and the Great Commission (Kevin DeYoung and Greg Gilbert)*
- *Ministries of Mercy: The Call of the Jericho Road (Timothy Keller)*

Online
- *How Do Word and Deed Ministry Fit Together for a Church?* gospelshapedchurch.org/resources511
- *How to Start a Mercy Ministry in your Church:* gospelshapedchurch.org/resources512
- *The Gospel and the Poor:* gospelshapedchurch.org/resources513
- *Mercy Ministry:* gospelshapedchurch.org/resources514
- *If Christ Predicted War, May Christians Pray for Peace?* gospelshapedchurch.org/resources515
- *What's Universal and Particular, Already and Not Yet?* gospelshapedchurch.org/resources516
- *The Power of the Gospel's 'Already' and 'Not Yet' for Right Now:* gospelshapedchurch.org/resources517

LEADER'S REFLECTIONS

SESSION 2:

JUSTICE: WRONGS MADE RIGHT

LAST SESSION WE LOOKED AT GOD'S PROMISE OF A
FUTURE WORLD MADE WHOLE AND BEAUTIFUL. BUT
WHAT DOES GOD WANT HIS PEOPLE TO DO AS WE WAIT,
LIVING IN THE TENSION BETWEEN THE "NOW" AND THE
"NOT YET"? IN THIS SESSION, WE'LL HEAR GOD'S CALL
TO HIS PEOPLE TO "DO JUSTICE" – TO WORK TO MAKE
RIGHT THE WRONGS OF OUR WORLD.

TALK OUTLINE

2.1 ● Once we are saved, what does God desire for us? To pray and read the Bible? Yes—but that's not all. He desires us to struggle for *shalom*.

2.2 ● **GOD HATES EMPTY RELIGION** *Amos 5:21-23*
  • Through Amos, God rebukes his people's empty religiosity.
  • We have hypocrisy too. But what if Amos 5 applied to us? The true test of our faith is whether we treat others with justice and compassion.

● **GOD LOVES JUSTICE** *Amos 5:24*
  • God wants his people to be characterized by **abundant justice** and **consistent righteousness**. Like water, justice is essential and refreshing.
  • There are two ends of the spectrum: Christians who focus on individual spirituality to the exclusion of social justice; and those who focus on social renewal to the exclusion of personal devotion and evangelism. But **God desires neither faithless justice nor justice-less faith**.

2.3 ● **DOING JUSTICE** *Psalm 146:5-9*
  • **Penal justice** punishes those who have done wrong. **Protective justice** ensures fairness flourishes and gives the vulnerable their due.
  • In Psalm 146 God is concerned for the oppressed, prisoners, the blind, the bowed down, the righteous, immigrants, widows and the fatherless.
  • To establish *shalom*, God must deal with sin. But how can a just God forgive the guilty? This is the **paradox of justice**.
  • The death of Christ satisfied God's penal justice and extends God's protective justice to those who take refuge in Jesus.

● **THE PURSUIT OF JUSTICE**
  • How are you being called to make wrongs right in your community? Who is oppressed, imprisoned, sick, an outsider, widowed or fatherless?
  • Why seek to make wrongs right? Because God has reconciled us to himself in Jesus—we do justice because God does justice.

You can download a full transcript of these talks at
WWW.GOSPELSHAPEDCHURCH.ORG/MERCY/TALKS

JUSTICE: WRONGS MADE RIGHT

* Ask *the group members to turn to Session 2 on page 33 of the Handbook.*

Discuss

What comes into your mind when you hear the word "justice"?

This starter question is to help people begin to think about the topic of justice. However, if group members only think quite narrowly about penal justice, you may want to widen the discussion yourself by including examples of social justice, such as how immigrants are treated or the poor provided for.

Think about the people in your neighborhood. Do you think they would associate your church or group with caring about justice? Why / why not?

This question will open up two issues: first, what areas of justice your church or group is currently involved in and, second, whether or not these are visible to your local community.

▶ **WATCH DVD 2.1 (2 min 8 sec) OR DELIVER TALK 2.1 (see page 52)**

* *Encourage the group to make notes as they watch the DVD or listen to the talk. There is space for notes on page 35 of the Handbook.*

☛ **AMOS 5:21-23**

> [21] *I hate, I despise your feasts,*
> *and I take no delight in your solemn assemblies.*
> [22] *Even though you offer me your burnt offerings and grain offerings,*
> *I will not accept them;*
> *and the peace offerings of your fattened animals,*
> *I will not look upon them.*

23 Take away from me the noise of your songs;
  to the melody of your harps I will not listen.

Discuss

These words were written nearly 2,800 years ago. Who do you think they apply to today?

> Try not to direct your group in how they answer this question. You're not looking for a "correct" answer—the aim is for people to become familiar with this passage, and to begin to think how it may apply, before it is then unpacked in Talk 2.2.

▶ **WATCH DVD 2.2** (7 min 28 sec) **OR DELIVER TALK 2.2** (see page 52)

* *Encourage the group to make notes as they watch the DVD or listen to the talk. There is space for notes on page 36 of the Handbook.*

Discuss

The way the Israelites were acting in Amos 5:21-23 can be described as "empty religiosity." In what way was their religious activity "empty," and how did God respond to it?

> "Religiosity" is an umbrella term for someone's religious activity, dedication and belief, often particularly applied to those aspects that are visible to others. But the religious activity of the Israelites was "empty." It looked right from the outside, but the Lord sees the heart (1 Samuel 16:7)—and what he saw in the hearts of the Israelites led him to reject their feasts and offerings.

☛ AMOS 5:24

> *24 But let justice roll down like waters,*
>   *and righteousness like an ever-flowing stream.*

What do we learn about justice from this verse?

* The Lord compares justice to water, which is so vital for life that we cannot exist

without it. Godly justice is equally vital for all people.

- Water is refreshing and attracts thirsty people. In the same way, godly justice attracts and invites people (whereas injustice repels and drives away).
- Water also cleans things, getting rid of dirt and stains, and restoring them to how they were intended to be. Right justice restores people and societies to what God intended for them.
- Justice and righteousness are compared to rolling, ever-flowing waters. In the same way, God's justice is intended to be constantly flowing. God himself is always right and just. In the same way, his people should constantly reflect his justice to the world.

"God desires neither faithless justice nor justice-less faith." While this sentence describes two extremes, the reality is often more subtle. In what ways do you see these two alternatives play out in your own experience?

"Faithless justice" may occur when people and churches are more concerned about social matters than they are about personal devotion. Social action can become an end in itself, rather than a reflection of God's perfectly just character, and of his work in our hearts by his Spirit to make us more and more like him.

"Justice-less faith" can happen when we give so much of our time to developing our own relationship with God (e.g. through personal Bible-reading, meeting with other Christians for Bible study, listening to online sermons) that we have no time left to spend with people in our neighborhood or to show practical care for them.

▶ **WATCH DVD 2.3** (8 min 14 sec) **OR DELIVER TALK 2.3** (see page 52)

* *Encourage the group to make notes as they watch the DVD or listen to the talk. There is space for notes on page 38 of the Handbook.*

👉 **PSALM 146:5-9**

⁵ *Blessed is he whose help is the God of Jacob,*
   whose hope is in the LORD his God,
⁶ *who made heaven and earth,*
   the sea, and all that is in them,
who keeps faith forever;

7 who executes justice for the oppressed,
   who gives food to the hungry.
The LORD sets the prisoners free;
8 the LORD opens the eyes of the blind.
The LORD lifts up those who are bowed down;
   the LORD loves the righteous.
9 The LORD watches over the sojourners;
   he upholds the widow and the fatherless,
   but the way of the wicked he brings to ruin.

Discuss

Discuss the questions raised in the talk (printed below). If you don't have time to discuss them all, choose two or three categories where you think you or your church may be weak.

Verse 7, the oppressed:

- Who in your church or neighborhood is experiencing vocational, financial, or relational hardship? How can you or your church address their needs?

Verse 7, prisoners:

- Are there those in your community who are literally imprisoned? Not just those in jail, but perhaps housebound or subject to domestic slavery? How might you and your church witness to the freedom of the gospel? How might you act as an advocate for the well-being of those that society has chosen to forget?

Verse 8, the blind (the sick):

- Who in your community or church is in need of physical assistance? How can you help to alleviate their suffering, whether permanent or temporary, and help them back toward health in its widest sense?

Verse 9, the sojourners (the outsiders):

- Are there those in your community who are not at "home" for one reason or another? They may be literally homeless, or have immigrated from another country, or are simply a community outsider. The question is: how can we make space for them in the warm, rather than leave them out in the cold?

Verse 9, the widows and fatherless:

- Who in your community experiences personal difficulty because of their relational situation? Are there single, divorced, or widowed people in need of assistance or friendship? Are there children who need physical, emotional and relational support and encouragement?

Beyond your neighborhood:

- The five sets of questions above all apply to your local community, but sometimes we will want to think more widely than that. What kind of issues do you think it is legitimate for Christians to campaign and fight for on the national stage, or internationally? How can you encourage those things to happen in your church, in a way that keeps a gospel perspective on the whole ministry?

NOTE: It would be easy to discuss the above issues but then do nothing further. Make a note of the ideas your group come up with, and plan what you will do next to start putting them into action. Depending on your situation, the first step may be to discuss your group's suggestions with your church leadership.

Pray

"God's justice is beautifully on display in the gospel. We see how seriously he takes sin, and how much he desires to embrace sinners. In Jesus, he does both."

Thank God for displaying his justice in the gospel.

Look again at your answers on pages 39 and 40. Ask God to help you put these into action.

DAILY BIBLE DEVOTIONALS

Remind group members about the daily devotionals they can do at home over the course of the next week. This week the devotionals take you through a variety of passages from Old and New Testaments that show that God has a heart of justice. To pursue justice ourselves, wherever we find it, is to be like our Father in heaven.

SERMONS

OPTION ONE: PSALM 146

Stephen focuses on elements of this passage in his DVD presentation, and you could expand upon it in a longer sermon.

OPTION TWO: AMOS 5:4-15

This is the passage the Bible study and most of the main session is based on, which could also be expanded upon in a sermon.

OPTION THREE: JOHN 8:1-11

This passage is not mentioned in the main material, but provides us with a powerful picture of how the Lord Jesus spoke out against an injustice:
- The Jewish leaders are being manipulative and "using" the woman for their own ends. Where was the man also caught in adultery?
- Jesus speaks out against the injustice through a direct attack on the leaders, and deals in mercy toward the woman, though not condoning her sin.
- We should speak out against injustice wherever we find it, not being fearful of exposing false motives in others (see Proverbs 31:8-9).

If one of your Sunday sermons is to be based on the theme of this session, church members will find a page to write notes on the sermon on page 51 of their Handbooks.

BIBLE STUDY

AIM: In the main teaching session this week, we thought about how God's sense of justice and "rightness" springs from his love for what he has created. In particular, we saw that working to make the world right, wherever we find unfairness, pleases God, who loves justice. This Bible study on Amos 5 aims to show how much God hates the oppression of the poor, and in particular, hates false religion in his people who do not care for the needs of the poor and oppressed.

Discuss

From an early age, children will complain: "It's not fair!" Why do you think this sense of justice is so powerful in us?

When we experience injustice, it very quickly attacks our sense of worth. They have got more than you because they are more favored/loved. You have got less than them because you are worth less. In one way "It's not fair" is a cry for us to be valued equally with others.

How does our sense of justice quickly go wrong?

- We very quickly learn how to use a claim of injustice for our own ends. We will exaggerate the injustice done to us, but minimize the injustices experienced by others, or the way we have not been fair to others.
- We want to escalate the punishment people receive when they wrong us. We are not very good at making the punishment fit the crime.
- We can just "give up" because of the overwhelming size of the problem. The scale of injustice seems so great; the problems of the world seem so wide; the complexity of the issues seems so deep that we fold our hands and say, "Why bother?" This is understandable.
- We can adopt a narrow view of our responsibilities. We may practice justice within our own limited sphere, but be unconcerned about it elsewhere.

If you have time, or feel that it is suitable for your group, you might invite one or two to share an example of when they were treated unjustly, and how it felt. The key thing to draw from this is the disparity between how we feel at unjust treatment, and our relative lack of empathy for those who are likewise treated. Don't let this discussion dominate the time—get on to reading the Bible!

👉 **READ AMOS 5:4-15**

> [15] *Hate evil, and love good, and establish justice in the gate;*
> *it may be that the LORD, the God of hosts,*
> *will be gracious to the remnant of Joseph.*

1. What aspects of God's character are underlined in this passage?

- He is the life-giver to those who seek him (v 4, 6).
- He is the judge of his people (v 6).
- He is the creator and sustainer of the universe (v 8). He is responsible for making their crops grow and for their wealth.
- He sees into the hearts of men and women—he knows our sins (v 12).
- He is merciful (v 15).

How do God's people stack up against this list?

Woefully:
- They despise the truth, and hate having their sins exposed and judged in court (v 10).
- They steal grain from the poor, and abuse them (v 11).
- They pervert the course of justice by oppression, bribery and manipulation (v 12).

2. What is the point being made in verse 13? Why is that so terrible?

Things are so bad—so unjust—that people don't even bother to complain about it. *What's the point in saying anything? It will only get us into more trouble.* When things have got that bad, a society is in a terrible place—there is no justice to be had anywhere. In other parts of Scripture, we hear of people crying out to the Lord for justice. Not here. Is the greater problem therefore that because the people who are perpetrating the injustice are supposed to be followers of the Lord, God has lost his reputation as the just God who will act to save the oppressed? This last point may be stretching it a little, but it's worth discussing with the group the temptation for us to do and say nothing, and to just "live with it." Those who stood out against slavery, for example, were often at the start lone voices against an (sometimes Christian) establishment that was happy with the status quo.

3. What appeal is made to the people in v 14-15? Why is that so generous?

They must repent on a personal level—hate evil, love good—but also on a structural level in their society. The courts must be reformed so that they deliver what they are supposed to: justice. This is incredibly generous, because God offers the people what they have never offered to anyone else. If God were to offer them justice, they would be swept away (v 9, 11). Instead he offers mercy, forgiveness, life—the very things they withheld from the poor.

 READ AMOS 5:21-24

> ²¹ *I hate, I despise your feasts,*
> *and I take no delight in your solemn assemblies.*

4. How does God view their religion? Why does he take their failings so seriously?

God hates everything about their religion—their services, singing and sacrifices are utterly loathsome for him. He will not listen to what they say to him. They are hypocrites. Worst of all, they are bringing the Lord God himself into disrepute by their covenant breaking. Israel was supposed to be a light to the nations (Isaiah 42:6). Outsiders were supposed to look at Israel and see a people and a place that were a delight to live among and in, where justice and peace reigned, and so come to worship the living God (we see this happening, for example, when the Queen of Sheba visits Solomon; see 1 Kings 10:4-9). But they had become just like the nations around them. Nothing special, nothing God-honoring about them. And in the context, their perversion of justice is the central hypocrisy that makes their worship disgusting to God.

How does the vehemence of this language make you feel? What should it lead us to do?

We should be very concerned about this! We often pride ourselves on the quality of our meetings, our music, or our messages. But these things are valueless unless we have the same concern for justice that the Lord has. Worse than that, "sound" or enthusiastic worship will actually condemn us if we lack God's passion to be fair to the poor, and not oppress them.

5. What might a Christian believer, and a church, that is working to realize verse 24 look like?

The image is one of clean, refreshing water that is ongoing, life-giving and unstoppable. Just as plant and animal life flourishes where there is water, so human life flourishes where there is justice and righteousness. For individuals, it speaks of a commitment to truth-telling, and making efforts to be fair in all their dealings with others—in business, in our families and in our personal relationships.

You may remember that this verse was part of Martin Luther King's famous "I have a dream" speech. Central issues of justice or lack of it will be different in different cultures and at different times. If you have time, and it is relevant for you, you might ask how the group thinks your country is doing in respect to King's 50-year old dream (please don't let this discussion dominate the proceedings!).

How does James 1:27 confirm that this is part of Christian discipleship?

Widows and orphans were the most vulnerable people in the ancient world—without a protector or a voice, and at the mercy of others. Christians are called to act as their protectors, to ensure they are dealt with justly and mercifully. This is "true religion," which God loves.

Apply

FOR YOURSELF: Discuss in what common ways you are tempted to act unjustly in your families, at work, or in the wider community. How can you let justice roll on like a river in your lives?

IN YOUR NATION: In what ways can you personally impact and fight injustice on a national and international level?

FOR YOUR CHURCH: How can a church fellowship live out verse 24 in its congregational life? Be very practical!

Pray

FOR YOUR GROUP: Pray that you would have a deeper understanding of how deep and wide God's love of justice and righteousness is. Use your answers to question 2 to inform your prayers.

FOR YOURSELF: If you are facing injustice or oppression yourself, pray for those who are responsible, and cry to God for justice.

FOR YOUR CHURCH: Pray that as individuals, and as a church, you would have a growing commitment to justice in the world, and so please God as you practice true religion.

FURTHER READING

> *Contrary to popular opinion, with God there is no such thing as mere forgiveness. There is only justice.*
> **Jerry Bridges**

> *If a person has grasped the meaning of God's grace in his heart, he will do justice. If he doesn't live justly, then he may say with his lips that he is grateful for God's grace, but in his heart he is far from him …*
> *Grace should make you just.*
> **Timothy Keller**

> *Even if I am a model of personal righteousness, that does not excuse my participation in social evil. The man who is faithful to his wife while he exercises bigotry toward his neighbor is no better than the adulterer who crusades for social justice. What God requires is justice both personal and social.*
> **R. C. Sproul**

Books

- *Urban Ministry: The Kingdom, the City & the People of God* (Harvie Conn and Manuel Ortiz)
- *To Live in Peace: Biblical Faith and the Changing Inner City* (Mark Gornik)
- *Generous Justice: How God's Grace Makes Us Just* (Timothy Keller)
- *God's Love Compels Us*, chapter 7 "Jesus and Justice" (Stephen Um)

Online

- *Nothing Less Than Justice:* gospelshapedchurch.org/resources521
- *Why All Christians Must Seek Public Justice:* gospelshapedchurch.org/resources522
- *How Should We Talk About Justice and the Gospel?* gospelshapedchurch.org/resources523
- *Generous Justice* (video): gospelshapedchurch.org/resources524
- *Are You Sure You Want God's Justice?* gospelshapedchurch.org/resources525

LEADER'S REFLECTIONS

SESSION 3:

LOVE: THE HEART OF COMPASSION

"A LIFE WITHOUT LOVE IS LIKE A SUNLESS GARDEN WHEN THE FLOWERS ARE DEAD," SAID THE WRITER OSCAR WILDE. ALL OF US LIKE THE IDEA OF LOVE – BUT IN REALITY, LOVING PEOPLE IS DIFFICULT AND COSTLY. IN THIS SESSION YOU'LL EXPLORE WHAT THE BIBLE SAYS ABOUT WHAT LOVE IS, WHERE IT COMES FROM, AND HOW TO PUT IT INTO PRACTICE.

TALK OUTLINE

3.1 ● Who doesn't like the idea of love? But there's a gap between **the ideal and the real**—the way we think things should be, and the way we're able to be.

● **HOW NOT TO LOVE** *1 John 3:11-18*
  • Don't love like Cain, who murdered his brother Abel (v 12). *Briefly retell the story from Genesis 4.*
  • Why did Cain do it? Because he was "of the evil one."
  • John gives us a **binary** way of seeing the world. People are either "of the evil one" or "of God"; death/life; hatred/love; self-love/love of others.
  • This black-and-white view of reality makes modern people uncomfortable. But it actually helps us navigate life in the "gray areas."
  • Death is at work in our hearts too (v 17)—it looks like self-interest, indifference, apathy and the absence of compassion.

3.2 ● **THE LIFE OF LOVE** *1 John 3:14-18*
How to we pass from death to life? Through Christ's death and resurrection. Love is the evidence of resurrection life (v 14). But what does the life of love look like?
  • **Self-sacrifice (v 16):** we're called to love as Christ loved us.
  • **Empathy (v 17):** a willingness to enter another's pain; a gut-level softness. The opposite is apathy—a gut-level callousness.
  • **Compassion (v 18):** actively doing something to help those in need.

3.3 ● **THE STRUGGLE TO LOVE** *1 John 3:19-24*
  • When we hear this call to love, we quickly see our own failing (v 19-20).
  • We need reassurance: **"God knows everything,"** yet he does not condemn us, because of Jesus. This is the truth we must preach to ourselves.
  • God doesn't apathetically ignore us; in Christ he **empathetically** embraces us.
  • Jesus experienced injustice to extend God's **compassion** to us.
  • Our hearts condemn us, but his heart vindicates us. *clear of blame or suspicion*

● **CONCLUSION:** God calls us to believe and love (v 23-24). How? The life of love is brought about by the Lord of love, who takes up residence in us.

You can download a full transcript of these talks at
WWW.GOSPELSHAPEDCHURCH.ORG/MERCY/TALKS

LOVE: THE HEART OF COMPASSION

● *Ask the group members to turn to Session 3 on page 53 of the Handbook.*

Discuss

 **1 JOHN 3:11-18**

> *11 For this is the message that you have heard from the beginning, that we should love one another. 12 We should not be like Cain, who was of the evil one and murdered his brother. And why did he murder him? Because his own deeds were evil and his brother's righteous. 13 Do not be surprised, brothers, that the world hates you. 14 We know that we have passed out of death into life, because we love the brothers. Whoever does not love abides in death. 15 Everyone who hates his brother is a murderer, and you know that no murderer has eternal life abiding in him.*
>
> *16 By this we know love, that he laid down his life for us, and we ought to lay down our lives for the brothers. 17 But if anyone has the world's goods and sees his brother in need, yet closes his heart against him, how does God's love abide in him? 18 Little children, let us not love in word or talk but in deed and in truth.*

Underline or circle the word "love" every time it occurs in the passage above. Whom does John say we are to love, and how?

- v 11: Love one another
- v 14: Love the brothers (fellow believers, both male and female)
- v 16: Love by laying down our lives for other believers (placing them first)
  placing your-self aside
- v 18: Love "in deed and in truth" (not just by what we say)

NOTE: Verse 12 refers to the Old Testament account of Cain and Abel (Genesis 4:1-16). If you think some of your group will be unfamiliar with this story, you may want to briefly summarize it for them.

WATCH DVD 3.1 (6 min 47 sec) **OR DELIVER TALK 3.1** (see page 70)

* *Encourage the group to make notes as they watch the DVD or listen to the talk. There is space for notes on page 56 of the Handbook.*

Discuss

"1 John gives us a binary way of seeing the world. People are either 'of the evil one' (v 12) or 'of God.'" How is this contrast seen in the account of Cain and Abel (v 12)?

* Cain: was of the evil one, murdered his brother, his own deeds were evil.
* Abel: his deeds were righteous.

It is easy to think we are nothing like Cain, but how does verse 15 define a murderer?

"Everyone who hates his brother is a murderer."

This may sound too extreme to members of your group, so look together at Jesus' words in Matthew 5:21-22. Whenever we hate, insult or are angry with a fellow Christian, we are showing the same heart disease that Cain showed. And a heart full of hate and anger is "of the evil one" (1 John 3:12).

WATCH DVD 3.2 (4 min 38 sec) **OR DELIVER TALK 3.2** (see page 70)

* *Encourage the group to make notes as they watch the DVD or listen to the talk. There is space for notes on page 57 of the Handbook.*

Discuss

Self-sacrifice (v 16): "By this we know love, that he laid down his life for us, and we ought to lay down our lives for the brothers."

Most of us will not need to die for the sake of our fellow Christians, though in some circumstances that may be required. How else can you "lay down your life" for others in your church?

[Handwritten notes: · stopping + helping though you are busy even · Taking responsibility/ownership for your actions - not blaming or making excuses involving others even if they are true. · talking to new people]

Self-sacrifice can involve both big and small sacrifices on our part (and sometimes it's the small ones we find hardest to make!). Encourage group members to suggest concrete examples of things they can do, rather than just general attitudes. What might they have to give up from their life (e.g. time, money, experiences, possessions) for the sake of someone else?

Empathy (v 17): *"But if anyone has the world's goods and sees his brother in need, yet closes his heart against him, how does God's love abide in him?"*

When do you find it easy to empathize with the needs of others? When are you at risk of "closing your heart" against them?

> *When I've gone through the same.*
>
> *When they don't help themselves, + if they are needy.*

John is writing about our Christian brothers and sisters in this passage. When do we find it easy to be empathetic or apathetic to members of our own church family? Times when we risk "closing our hearts" against them may include:

- when the same need comes up again and again
- when the person asking for help is annoying
- when they don't thank us for helping them
- when we think someone else should be doing it rather than us
- when we have our own problems to focus on.

Is it different when we hear of Christians in need in other countries (or even in other parts of our own country)?

Compassion (v 18): *"Little children, let us not love in word or talk but in deed and in truth."*

When do you find yourself talking about fellow believers who need help? What can you do to ensure that your "talk" works itself out "in deed and in truth"?

Try and encourage everyone in your group to think of at least one situation where they will be talking about Christians in need. What can they put in place to help move on from just talking to helpful action? If the most likely place you'll be talking about these things is in the group you are meeting in today, how can you make sure you remind each other of the importance of putting these things into practice? *Setting dates, reminders and challenges.*

NOTE: Read 1 John 3:19-24 together before the final DVD segment or talk so that your group is familiar with the passage.

1 JOHN 3:19-24

¹⁹ By this we shall know that we are of the truth and reassure our heart before him; ²⁰ for whenever our heart condemns us, God is greater than our heart, and he knows everything. ²¹ Beloved, if our heart does not condemn us, we have confidence before God; ²² and whatever we ask we receive from him, because we keep his commandments and do what pleases him. ²³ And this is his commandment, that we believe in the name of his Son Jesus Christ and love one another, just as he has commanded us. ²⁴ Whoever keeps his commandments abides in God, and God in him. And by this we know that he abides in us, by the Spirit whom he has given us.

▶ **WATCH DVD 3.3** (6 min 59 sec) **OR DELIVER TALK 3.3** (see page 70)

* *Encourage the group to make notes as they watch the DVD or listen to the talk. There is space for notes on page 58 of the Handbook.*

Discuss

"John knows that when we hear the call to a life of love—to empathy, compassion and self-sacrifice—our hearts are going to condemn us as unfeeling, selfish self-pleasers."

How is the gospel both the answer to our self-condemnation and also the spur to love others more fully?

* Verse 20 tells us that "God is greater than our heart, and he knows everything." He sees even more clearly than we do our selfish thoughts and actions, and lack of compassion. But if we are Christians, then God does not condemn us for these things because they have been paid for by the blood of his Son. Through Christ we have been forgiven—our hearts are washed clean (Hebrews 10:22).
* The love of Christ, shown especially in his death for our sin, should spur us on to love others. This was Jesus' own command to his followers: "This is my commandment, that you love one another as I have loved you" (John 15:12).

It's easy to get to the end of a session like this thinking, "I must be more loving," but then not do anything about it. Write down three things you can put into practice this week:

1. To show love to someone in your family or a close friend *– spend time with them. I usually pick Luke over them :/*
2. To show love to someone from your church family *– make a dinner/dessert*

3. To show love to someone in your neighborhood *acknowledge + smile*

> Encourage everyone in your group to write something after all three questions. Perhaps you can agree as a group that you will ask each other how you got on the next time you meet.

How will you motivate yourself to do these things (v 16)?

> Our motivation isn't thinking about the deeds, or the love we are showing as we do them, but to focus on Jesus. His self-sacrifice for us is what motivates us to show self-sacrificial love to others.

Pray

> *23 And this is his commandment, that we believe in the name of his Son Jesus Christ and love one another, just as he commanded us. 24 Whoever keeps his commandments abides in God, and God in him. And by this we know that he abides in us, by the Spirit whom he has given us. (1 John 3:23-24)*

> Do you believe in Jesus Christ (v 23)? If so, this faith is a gift from God. Thank him for it.

> How much do you love one another (v 23)? Ask God to grow this love in your heart, and to help you work it out in your everyday actions.

> Thank God that he abides in you, and you in him (v 24). He has made his home in you; and you have found your home forever in him. Ask him to help you remember this powerful truth as you go about your day, and to more fully reflect his love to others as a result.

DAILY BIBLE DEVOTIONALS

This week's daily Bible devotionals take a long look at perhaps the most famous passage in the Bible about love: 1 Corinthians 13. The aim is to deepen our understanding and give shape to the meaning of love in the Bible, and show how it is so much greater and more far-reaching than most people think.

SERMONS

OPTION ONE: 1 JOHN 3:11-24

This is the passage Stephen looks at in his DVD presentation, which could be expanded upon in a sermon.

OPTION TWO: 1 JOHN 4:7-21

This is the passage the Bible study is based on (see next page), which could also be expanded upon in a sermon.

OPTION THREE: DEUTERONOMY 10:12-19

This passage is not mentioned in this material, but it shows us that the call to love has always been a part of God's command to his people, especially to love those who are different from us.
- God calls his people to love him and be obedient to all his commands.
- This love flows out of who he is, the sovereign Lord of all, and what he has done—he has saved his people.
- This love is particularly directed at foreigners, the poor and the dispossessed. A failure to love them is a failure to understand where we have come from.

Church members will find a page to write notes on the sermon on page 71 of their Handbooks.

BIBLE STUDY

AIM: The origins of genuine love, and the difficulties we have in expressing it, were the focus of the main session this week—seen from 1 John 3. In this Bible study, we think about the following chapter, and what the expression of genuine Christian love looks like.

Discuss

"How can you tell if someone really loves you?" How do you think most people would answer this question?

> Encourage group members not to generalize but to talk about the opinions of people they speak to on a regular basis. There will be a range of answers, but they will often focus on the feelings of the person in question, and the way they talk and relate to others. They will often not be concerned with their actions. As people give their answers, try to summarize the core of what they are saying, and then point out the distinction.
>
> Come back to this question at the end, by way of summary, but add the question: How can you tell that someone loves Jesus?

 READ 1 JOHN 4:7-21

> *7 Beloved, let us love one another, for love is from God, and whoever loves has been born of God and knows God. 8 Anyone who does not love does not know God, because God is love. 9 In this the love of God was made manifest among us, that God sent his only Son into the world, so that we might live through him.*

1. **Why should we love one another (v 7-12)?**

   John's argument is simply this:
   - God is love.
   - We are of God.
   - Therefore we should love.

2. *How* should we love one another?

We love because we are born of the God who is love. So our love should be like God's love. And the supreme expression of God's love is the cross. Our love should be infused with the same qualities that took Christ to the cross.

What does the cross reveal about God's love?

- God's love is costly (he gave his only son).
- God's love is undeserved (he did not wait for us to love him).
- God's love is effective or practical (he gives us life and atonement).
- Jesus did not mind being humbled (our love should not mind taking a lowly path).

Try to tease these qualities out of your group, and make them real with examples. The undeserved angle is particularly important. We tend to pick and choose who we love, based on some merit in them, or some advantage for us. Jesus died for his enemies, when they could not care less.

3. What amazing claim is made in verse 12?

We cannot see God. But in a very real and tangible way, the invisible God is made visible through our love as Christians.

What implications does this have for our outreach and pastoral care as a church?

We display something of the gospel message through our relationships with one another in the Christian community (see John 13 v 34-35 and 17 v 23). We attract people to the Christian message by reflecting something of God's character. When, for example, other Christians doubt God's goodness or control, the loving life of the body of Christ is a visible and tangible reminder to them of God's love through our actions, as well as our words.

Likewise, outsiders will experience the distinct quality of Christian love, which is thoughtful, intelligent, and practical, when they spend time with us. It is a profoundly evangelistic experience for many people. The implication is that we should seek opportunities for non-believers to just "hang out" with Christians in some way, not necessarily just inviting them to hear gospel messages.

4. **How can we know for sure that we are a genuine Christian (v 13-16)? Is it possible to tell if someone else is a genuine believer? Why / why not?**

- The Spirit testifies that we are Christians (v 13). There are many things that this could include:
  - The inner witness of God's spirit in our hearts calling God "Father" (see Romans 8:15-16)
  - The confidence to believe and assert that "Jesus is Lord" (1 Corinthians 12:3)
  - The evidence of a changed sensitivity to sin. (He is the *Holy* Spirit!)
  - The evidence of growing love for God and others.
- True Christians believe the truth about Jesus (v 14).
- This shows we are true Christians because acknowledging the truth is a sign of God at work in our lives (v 15).
- True Christians love one another because they are children of the God of love (v 16).
- Sometimes these qualities—marks of the Spirit's work in us— are more visible to others than to ourselves. We can discern these encouraging signs in others, but it can never really be "proof."

Is love for others or belief in the truth the most important sign that someone follows correct teaching? How are the two connected?

Point the group to John's definition of love in verse 9 and John's definition of truth in verse 14.

Some people suggest love is more important than truth; others that truth is more important than love. But John defines love and truth in the same way: God sending his Son into the world to save us. They are bound together. If you do not show love, you clearly don't know the truth. If you do not believe the truth, it is impossible to love.

Love is actively doing something that will be for the good of others, but we will only know what that truly is if we know the truth of the gospel.

Because truth is to be lived, if head knowledge has no effect on the way we act in the world, it shows we do not really know the truth.

Additional question: From these verses, how would you help a Christian who is plagued with doubts about whether they truly belong to Christ?

5. Where does genuine Christian love come from (v 19)? How can we grow in that love?

It comes from a direct response to the gospel. We will grow in love, the more we appreciate and understand how much Jesus loves us. That comes from a growing understanding of both how sinful we really are and how great God is.

How can love be commanded (v 21)? What are the implications for how we seek to grow our love?

- Sometimes, we just don't "feel it." At those times it's important that we remember that love is an obligation that we owe, regardless of how we instinctively feel.
- We can lose sight of God's love for us; we can struggle to love certain people at certain times because they are "unlovely" in some way to us. Knowing that it is a command from Jesus will enable us to "just do it" when we don't feel it.
- We should tell ourselves to love people; preach God's command to yourself.
- We can and should urge each other to love—and encourage each other with affirmation when we see people loving as Jesus did. How wonderful for someone to say to you, "When you did that, it reminded me of Jesus."

Summarize

How would you answer Question 1 after thinking about this passage? How would you answer the question: How can you tell that someone loves Jesus?

Apply

FOR YOURSELF AND YOUR CHURCH: Who do you find difficult to love, both as individuals and corporately as a church? How can you encourage each other to be more loving, both in quantity and quality?

Pray

FOR YOUR GROUP: Pray that you would understand God's love for you in Christ more deeply than ever. Pray that your love would be suffused with the knowledge and wisdom of Christ, as you reflect on his word.

FOR YOUR CHURCH: Pray that your love for each other would spill over into the world, and that those who spend time with you would see Jesus in your life, as you love others selflessly and with generosity.

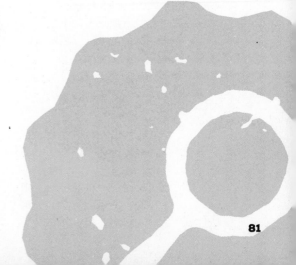

FURTHER READING

> *Biblical orthodoxy without compassion is surely the ugliest thing in the world.*
> **Francis Schaeffer**

> *If your heart is full of love, it will find vent; you will find or make ways enough to express your love in deeds. When a fountain abounds in water it will send forth streams.*
> **Jonathan Edwards**

> *One sin leads to another. Failure in our love to God always results in failure in our love to our neighbor.*
> **A. W. Pink**

Books
- *The Difficult Doctrine of the Love of God (D. A. Carson)*
- *God's Love: How the Infinite God Cares for His Children (R. C. Sproul)*
- *Gospel Centered Church: Becoming the Community God Wants You to Be (Steve Timmis and Tim Chester)*

Online
- *The Love That is Neither Easy Nor Natural:* gospelshapedchurch.org/resources531
- *We Need to Be Careful, but We Also Need to Care:* gospelshapedchurch.org/resources532
- *If We Love God Most, We Will Love Others Best:* gospelshapedchurch.org/resources533
- *It's Not Enough to Care About "The Poor":* gospelshapedchurch.org/resources534
- *Sacrificial Love Is the Key to the Christian Life:* gospelshapedchurch.org/resources535

LEADER'S REFLECTIONS

SESSION 4:

MERCY: HEARTS MADE SOFT

SO FAR WE'VE DISCOVERED THAT GOD DESIRES A WORLD
OF SHALOM; WE'VE SEEN HOW GOD CALLS HIS PEOPLE
TO WORK FOR JUSTICE; AND WE'VE BEEN CHALLENGED
TO LIVE A LIFE CHARACTERIZED BY SELF-GIVING LOVE.
IN THIS SESSION WE'LL TIE ALL THOSE IDEAS TOGETHER
AS WE LOOK AT THE THEME OF MERCY – AND REFRESH
OURSELVES IN THE FOUNTAIN OF MERCY: JESUS CHRIST.

TALK OUTLINE

4.1 • Mercy is **love in action** on behalf of **those in need**.

4.2 • THE SIGNIFICANCE OF MERCY *Matthew 25:31-46*
Mercy is not an optional supplement to the life of faith. It's for everyone.
- **Mercy is eternally significant (v 31):** what we do now has eternal significance.
- **Mercy is universally required (v 32):** Jesus judges "all the nations."
- **Mercy is the ultimate test (v 32):** we do not do mercy to *become* sheep; doing mercy is evidence *that we are* sheep. It is a litmus test of whether we have been truly shaped by the gospel.

• THE REALITY OF JUDGMENT
We're all searching for a paradoxical combination of justice and mercy. We all desire *shalom*—but there is no way that can happen unless injustice is addressed by a just judge. This is good news for those suffering injustice of any kind.

• THE PRACTICE OF MERCY
- The sheep are those who have experienced God's mercy and extend it to others.
- Both the sheep and the goats are surprised by Jesus' judgment! Mercy is the sheep's knee-jerk reaction (v 37-40); they are not keeping score. But the goats resort to self-justification (v 44-45). Their lack of fruit reveals a deeper issue.
- Remember, if your faith is in Christ, there is no need to fear judgment. You are a sheep of his pasture.

4.3 • RADICAL MERCY IN ACTION
- Doing mercy is not safe or comfortable. We can't just give money or volunteer occasionally; selfless love-in-action must become a way of life.
- How can we become this kind of person? We must turn to the **fountain of mercy**.
- On the cross Jesus was thirsty, a rejected outsider, and naked. He experienced the consequence of our spiritual sickness—death. He became the ultimate needy one in order to meet our ultimate need for mercy.
- As we see Jesus like this, we seek to become imitators of our great Shepherd. Mercy is the only possible response to his mercy to us.

You can download a full transcript of these talks at
WWW.GOSPELSHAPEDCHURCH.ORG/MERCY/TALKS

MERCY: HEARTS MADE SOFT

Discuss

Imagine if we started this session by asking each person to tell the group who they have shown mercy to in the last week. Would you want to answer the question? Why / why not?

Try not to get bogged down with issues of exactly *how* people have shown mercy, e.g. whether it's giving money to someone in need, or visiting a sick neighbor. The question asks "who" not "how." The idea is to start people thinking about whether they have shown mercy recently, and how they would feel if other people knew exactly what they have or haven't done. Possible answers might include: "It's private," "I'm embarrassed about how little I do," "I don't want to boast," "I don't want to be compared with other people," "It's not my job—we have a person/group at church to do that for us."

▶ **WATCH DVD 4.1** (3 min 49 sec) **OR DELIVER TALK 4.1** (see page 88)

* *Encourage the group to make notes as they watch the DVD or listen to the talk. There is space for notes on page 75 of the Handbook.*

👉 **MATTHEW 25:31-46**

31 When the Son of Man comes in his glory, and all the angels with him, then he will sit on his glorious throne. 32 Before him will be gathered all the nations, and he will separate people one from another as a shepherd separates the sheep from the goats. 33 And he will place the sheep on his right, but the goats on the left. 34 Then the King will say to those on his right, "Come, you who are blessed by my Father, inherit the kingdom prepared for you from the foundation of the world. 35 For I was hungry and you gave me food, I was thirsty and you gave me drink, I was a stranger and you welcomed me, 36 I was naked and you clothed me, I was sick and you visited me, I was in prison and you came to me." 37 Then the righteous will answer him, saying, "Lord, when did we see you hungry and feed you, or thirsty and give you drink? [38] And when did we see you a stranger and welcome you, or naked and clothe you? [39] And when did we see you sick or in prison and visit you?" [40] And the King will answer them, "Truly, I say to you, as you did it to one of the least of these my brothers, you did it to me."

[41] Then he will say to those on his left, "Depart from me, you cursed, into the eternal fire prepared for the devil and his angels. [42] For I was hungry and you gave me no food, I was thirsty and you gave me no drink, [43] I was a stranger and you did not welcome me, naked and you did not clothe me, sick and in prison and you did not visit me." [44] Then they also will answer, saying, "Lord, when did we see you hungry or thirsty or a stranger or naked or sick or in prison, and did not minister to you?" [45] Then he will answer them, saying, "Truly, I say to you, as you did not do it to one of the least of these, you did not do it to me." [46] And these will go away into eternal punishment, but the righteous into eternal life.

Discuss

This session builds on the details in Jesus' account of the sheep and the goats in Matthew 25:31-46. Use these verses to fill in the table below.

	Sheep	Goats
Where will Jesus put people (v 33)?	Sheep on his right	Goats on his left
How does Jesus describe them?	v 34: Blessed by his Father	v 41: Cursed
Where will they go?	v 34: The kingdom prepared for them from the foundation of the world	v 41: The eternal fire prepared for the devil and his angels
	v 46: Eternal life	v 46: Eternal punishment

	Sheep	Goats
What did they do /not do for Jesus?	**v 35 (3 things):** • Gave him food when hungry • Gave him drink when thirsty • Welcomed him when a stranger **v 36 (3 things):** • Clothed him when naked • Visited him when sick • Came to him in prison	**v 42 (2 things):** • Gave him no food when hungry • Gave him no drink when thirsty **v 43 (4 things):** • Did not welcome him when a stranger • Did not clothe him when naked • Did not visit him when sick • Did not visit him when in prison

When is this separation going to occur (v 31)?

When Jesus (he often called himself "the Son of Man") "comes in his glory, and all the angels with him," and is seated "on his glorious throne." In other words, when Jesus returns to judge the world.

▶ **WATCH DVD 4.2** (11 min 57 sec) **OR DELIVER TALK 4.2** (see page 88)

✱ *Encourage the group to make notes as they watch the DVD or listen to the talk. There is space for notes on page 78 of the Handbook.*

Discuss

Does Jesus list people's acts of mercy before or after he separates them into sheep and goats? Why does this matter?

- He lists their acts of mercy *after* separating them into sheep and goats.
- It matters because the acts of mercy are not the basis on which people are separated. Instead, they are the *evidence* that confirms which group each person belongs to. Jesus is saying that his sheep (his followers) do mercy. He is *not* saying that doing mercy is the way that goats become sheep.
- This truth could be put the other way round for emphasis: *If you are not doing acts of mercy, it is evidence that you are a goat, not a sheep.*

NOTE: The seriousness of the final judgment is clear from the destinations of the two groups. The sheep are heading to "eternal life," but the goats to "eternal punishment" (v 46). However, the definition of a sheep is based on what *Jesus* has done, not on what *we* have done. In the DVD, Stephen Um explains it like this: *"Throughout the book of Matthew, Jesus says that he was sent to gather lost sheep. He is the kind of shepherd who leaves the entire flock to pursue the one wandering sheep. In other words, **you are a sheep if Jesus finds you**—if he claims you for himself. And if Jesus finds you in his mercy, it is only natural that you would do mercy. We do not do mercy to earn acceptance and identity—we do mercy because we have been accepted and given a new identity."* So, if you and your group members are already putting your trust in Jesus, you do not need to fear the final judgment. You are already his sheep, and can look forward to eternal life with Christ.

Who are the sheep being merciful to (v 40)? Is that who you expected Jesus to be talking about?

- "One of the least of these my brothers." This means these acts of mercy are shown to Christian believers (both male and female).
- This passage is often applied to general acts of mercy shown to any- and every-one. For example, you may have heard Mother Theresa quoted as saying of the poor that "each one of them is Jesus in disguise." However, while there are other biblical texts that do teach the need to help needy people of all religions or none (e.g. Luke 10:25-37; Galatians 6:10), the focus of this passage is on caring for the *Christian* needy.

"Mercy is the mark of a church that has been shaped by the gospel." **If someone came to visit your church or group for the first time, or found out about it some other way (e.g. asking around, checking out your website), would they say it is marked by mercy? How would they know? What about someone who lives in the neighborhood, but isn't a member of the church? Would their view be different?**

Additional questions to help your group think about this could be: What would a visitor observe or hear during a church service? Do you have any displays in your building that tell newcomers about any ministries of mercy? How about on your website? If someone came to your church needing help, either on a Sunday or midweek, would they know who to ask and/or what kind of help is available?

▶ **WATCH DVD 4.3** (6 min 5 sec) **OR DELIVER TALK 4.3** (see page 88)

* *Encourage the group to make notes as they watch the DVD or listen to the talk. There is space for notes on page 79 of the Handbook.*

Discuss

Look at your list on page 77 of the kinds of acts of mercy the sheep were doing. Which of these are you currently involved in, either as individuals or as a church? How could you add the others?

You could use the chart on page 77 as a checklist, checking the ones that are already happening and putting a star by the ones that are not. Then spend some time discussing those with stars by them. If you are short of time, choose at least two to discuss, and encourage group members to think about the others later on. You could also agree to spend the first few minutes of the next session finding out what people thought about any issues you don't have time to discuss in detail now.

What changes are you going to make as a result of this session?

You may want to give the group time to think about this individually and write down the changes they have decided to make privately. Some concrete actions might be: to pray about and review their involvement in acts of mercy; to encourage others to show mercy; and to be more proactive in offering to help others. Try to make sure there's time for them to do this now—if they leave it until later, it's far more likely that they won't do it!

NOTE: Look back at the action points you wrote down in Sessions 2 and 3 (pages 39-40 and 59-60). How are you getting on with those? Some of them might be added to your list above, to reinforce decisions you have already made.

Pray

"Jesus, the Good Shepherd, became a sheep and was slaughtered for us.
- *Because he went hungry, we are fed with the bread of life.*
- *Because he went thirsty, we drink living water.*
- *Because he became a stranger, we experience welcome.*
- *Because he was stripped naked, we are clothed with robes of righteousness.*
- *Because he was executed as a criminal, we are set free.*
- *Because he bore death, we experience life."*

Turn each of the points above into a prayer of thankfulness to Jesus, our Good Shepherd.

Now look at the action points you have listed above, and ask God to help you start to make them a reality this week.

DAILY BIBLE DEVOTIONALS

Do encourage your group members at the end of the main teaching session to keep studying, or start to study, the daily devotionals. This week, they take a careful look at the parable of the "Good Samaritan."

SERMONS

OPTION ONE: MATTHEW 25:31-46

This is the main passage Stephen looks at in his DVD presentation, which could be expanded upon in a sermon.

OPTION TWO: ACTS 6:1-7

This is the passage the Bible study is based on (see next page), which could also be expanded upon in a sermon.

OPTION THREE: MICAH 6:8

A famous Bible verse that shows what God requires of each of us:
- What does God count as really important? It is not the things we might think (v 6-7).
- When we do justice and mercy (and don't just think about it!), we are being like God, who is just and merciful. Mercy is love in action, which does not depend on whether we feel someone else deserves it or not.
- But justice and kindness (mercy) are nothing, unless they come from our humble walk with the Lord.

If one of your Sunday sermons is to be based on the theme of this session, church members will find a page to write notes on the sermon on page 91 of their Handbooks.

BIBLE STUDY

AIM: As we saw in the main session, mercy is "love in action on behalf of those in need." This Bible study aims to revisit some of the fundamental ideas from the main session, and to describe how the early church balanced the gospel call to provide for the poor and needy with maintaining a focus on the work of gospel outreach.

Discuss

Many churches struggle to work out how much energy to put into "mercy ministries" they may be involved in, as opposed to evangelism. This is not a new problem, as will be seen in this study on the early church.

Do you think your church is taking practical mercy and gospel evangelism seriously? Make a quick list of what your church does in each area. Do you think this is a healthy balance, or are you concerned that one is detracting from the other?

> The discussion here will be different for every church fellowship. You should consider not just the amount and time spent on each area of activity, but any sense of disquiet there might be among group members about the balance (or the absence of one or the other). No need to comment on the answers; just log where people are coming from in this discussion, and any fears and concerns there might be.
>
> You might add a follow-on question: *What happens when the balance goes wrong?*

👉 **READ ACTS 6:1-7**

> *¹ Now in these days when the disciples were increasing in number, a complaint by the Hellenists arose against the Hebrews because their widows were being neglected in the daily distribution.*

1. What was the practice of the early church in regard to the needy?

There was a daily distribution of food to widows—people who did not have a protector or provider to care for them. This appears to have been done as a centralized system, and was working well at one stage (see Acts 4:32-34). Providing for the poor was part of old covenant obligations, and something that Jesus himself practiced. Note that Judas kept the money bag used by Jesus and his disciples for a communal fund to give to the poor (John 12:4-6). This practice was clearly extended and organized in the early Jerusalem church. Paul also organized a widespread collection of money for needy Christians experiencing famine in Judea (2 Corinthians 9:5).

What situation had arisen? Why was it potentially so damaging?

It started as an issue of justice. The Greek widows were missing out on the distribution in favor of the Jewish women. The Hellenists complained to the Twelve. There were two dangers:

- *Division:* Injustice was forcing apart the Hebrew and Hellenistic believers from each other—this divide was a continuing struggle in the early church, with a number of potential flashpoints.
- *Distraction:* The mercy ministry to widows was threatening to prevent the Twelve from preaching and teaching.

2. What was the apostles' solution?

- *Involvement:* They took the matter to the whole church (v 2), and discussed their solution together.
- *Delegation:* They chose seven people full of the Spirit and wisdom to do this job.
- *Focus:* This enabled them to focus on their particular purpose: prayer and the ministry of the word.

What wrong steps could they have taken instead?

They avoided two problems that churches today often make:

- *Evangelism has to wait for mercy.* "Hey, we need to sort out this potentially divisive widow-starving issue that is preventing us from displaying the kingdom. Let's all get involved in it; the teaching can take a back seat for now. If God's people are not about mercy and service, then we're not about anything."
- *Mercy has to wait for evangelism.* "Look, we're a word-based ministry, so

that must come first. The rest will sort itself out organically. We must not be distracted from declaring the kingdom."

What is distinctive about the people they chose? What lessons are there in this for us?

When we delegate things, we often think about choosing "the practical people" to do a job like this—and yet, the apostles stipulate that this is clearly a spiritual task. Those who do it must be wise and Spirit-filled. Notice that they chose people who were:

- *gifted:* Stephen was clearly a very godly man, and a terrific preacher! (See Acts 7.) We ought not to assume that if we are godly and gifted at word ministries, then others should be taking the lead on mercy ministries.
- *diverse:* more of the names have Greek overtones than Jewish ones—perhaps they were concerned to make sure that the charge of injustice was put aside beyond any doubt. The inclusion of Nicolaus from Antioch is also significant. As a "proselyte" he is likely to have been non-Jewish by birth, but a convert to Judaism and then a follower of Jesus. He is the first recorded non-Jew, therefore, to be admitted into church leadership.
- *commissioned:* they were commissioned for the work by the Twelve. This work was not an "add on" to the church's gospel work, but an integral part of it that was recognized by the whole congregation.

3. What was the result of this change (v 7)? How did that happen?

Gospel growth. We can discern three possible factors that are important here:

- The Twelve were set free to preach and pray. For people to respond to the gospel, they must hear it (preaching). For people to respond to the gospel, God must open their eyes (prayer).
- The care that the disciples took of the widows, and the spiritual and practical manner in which it was done, may have added to the good reputation of this new sect within the community. It was certainly a work that "adorned" the gospel message.
- The fairness of the system would have particularly attracted Hellenistic Jews perhaps, although verse 7 makes specific mention of priests, who would have been Hebrew-speaking Jews.

SCAN-READ ACTS 6:7 – 7:60

⁸ And Stephen, full of grace and power, was doing great wonders and signs among the people. ⁹ Then some of those who belonged to the synagogue of the Freedmen (as it was called), and of the Cyrenians, and of the Alexandrians, and of those from Cilicia and Asia, rose up and disputed with Stephen.

4. What happened next? Why is it important for us to remember this?

- Stephen was persecuted and martyred—a man full of grace and the Holy Spirit, who humbly served needy widows!
- Some people may see our good works and glorify our Father in heaven (Matthew 5:16). Mercy ministries done well will serve gospel outreach. But others will hate the light, and not come to it, lest their evil works should be exposed (John 3:20).
- We should not expect praise from others for any mercy ministry we perform, nor assume that it will automatically bring gospel growth with it—it may bring persecution.
- Nonetheless, we must love and do good to others because it is the right thing to do, and a natural outcome of a gospel-centered life and church.

Apply

FOR YOUR CHURCH: Revisit the opening discussion question in light of what you have read in Acts. Is your answer still the same? How would you go about doing something to change it?

Try to make this a practical answer.
- If the group thinks that things are unfair or imbalanced, they should approach the church leadership with the question.
- We should dispel any idea that the two activities are somehow in competition with each other. The apostles found a solution that actually increased the focus on word ministry, while growing the fairness and provision of the mercy ministry. We should work to do the same, by involving more people in the work.
- Any solution must have "buy in" from the congregation.
- Any solution must also ensure that the work is done in a spiritual way, by spiritual people.

Pray

FOR YOUR CHURCH: Pray that you would discharge your responsibilities as a congregation to care for the needy in your church, and those in your wider community.

FOR YOUR COMMUNITY: Pray for gospel growth in and through your church, and for people to become genuine Christians.

FOR YOUR LEADERS: Pray for those who give themselves to preaching and prayer; and for those who give themselves to mercy ministries—that they would all be filled with the Spirit to do the work God has called them to.

FURTHER READING

> *God's mercy makes my faith;*
> *and my faith, my love,*
> *and my love, my works.*
> **William Tyndale**

> *Mercy is something we extend, not just something we intend.*
> **George Grant**

> *Yes, our deeds of mercy are a platform to help people believe the gospel, but that is not the primary reason for mercy. Mercy is ultimately a natural expression from those who already believe the gospel.*
> **Randy Smith**

Books

- *Good News to the Poor: Social Involvement and the Gospel (Tim Chester)*
- *Church in Hard Places: How the Local Church Brings Life to the Poor and Needy (Mez McConnell and Mike McKinley)*
- *Ministries of Mercy: The Call of the Jericho Road (Timothy Keller)*

Online

- The One Who Showed Mercy: gospelshapedchurch.org/resources541
- 5 Ways to Help the "Least of These" in the Church: gospelshapedchurch.org/resources542
- Scary Mercy: gospelshapedchurch.org/resources543
- A Conversation: Tim Keller, John Piper, D.A. Carson – Ministries of Mercy (video): gospelshapedchurch.org/resources544
- How Do You Reconcile God's Justice with His Mercy? gospelshapedchurch.org/resources545
- Thinking Through Your Church's Mercy Ministry gospelshapedchurch.org/resources546
- How to Start and Persevere with Inner-City Ministry gospelshapedchurch.org/resources547

LEADER'S REFLECTIONS

SESSION 5:

GENEROSITY: STEWARDING GOD'S MONEY

THIS SESSION IS ABOUT MONEY. FOR MOST OF US, IT'S A TOPIC WE'D RATHER NOT TALK ABOUT PUBLICLY. BUT FOR THE BIBLE-WRITER JAMES, IT'S A TOPIC HE TACKLES HEAD ON. IN THIS SESSION WE'LL BE CHALLENGED BY SOME UNCOMFORTABLE TRUTHS – BUT WE'LL ALSO BE WOWED BY GOD'S OVERFLOWING GENEROSITY.

TALK OUTLINE

5.1 Spurgeon said, "With some [Christians] the last part of their nature that ever gets sanctified is their pockets." Money has always been an issue for Christians!

- Not Given ours
- Not our identity
- Temporary

• THE TROUBLE WITH MONEY *James 2:1-10*

In this passage, James addresses money head on:

- **James makes money a public conversation:** it's not "our" money.
- **He makes money a moral matter:** there's a right and a wrong way to use it.
- **He strips money of its identity-making power:** it is God who provides our identity.

How did the early church end up like this? James reminds them of two things:

(1) Money is temporary (1:9-11): when we understand this, we hold wealth loosely. The only identity and security that matters is ours in Christ.

(2) Money comes from God (1:17): it's not our hard work or cleverness that got it for us—nor do we have the ultimate right to decide what is done with it.

5.2 • THE UNJUST USE OF MONEY *James 5:1-6*

In chapter 5, James highlights three facets of the unjust use of money:

- **Hoarding (v 2-3):** the rich store up wealth while the poor suffer—and the rich will face judgement. Today we easily become compulsive consumers, spending money on things that will corrode.
- **Fraud (v 4):** don't be a cheapskate to pad your own pockets. Do we consider the well-being of people who are part of the global system producing our goods?
- **Self-indulgence (v 5):** the sinfully rich are like fattened animals being led to slaughter. But Christians in the West seem to be just as self-indulgent and luxury-oriented as their neighbors. *Does your standard of living look any different?*

5.3 • THE GOSPEL AND MONEY

We are guilty, but God is generous! In Christ he pours out his mercy, gives of himself, and forgoes the luxuries of heaven to secure them for us. Our confidence is not in corroding riches but incorruptible grace. Three implications:

- **Hoarding is not an option:** it is *God's* money. Generosity is justice, not charity.
- **We will not defraud others:** God has ultimately provided for us in Christ.
- **Self-indulgence is not for us:** we can forgo luxury for the sake of others.

You can download a full transcript of these talks at
WWW.GOSPELSHAPEDCHURCH.ORG/MERCY/TALKS

GENEROSITY: STEWARDING GOD'S MONEY

Discuss

This session digs into various parts of the letter of James. Who was James writing to? (See James 1:1.)

"The twelve tribes in the Dispersion" (ESV)—or, in the NIV, "The twelve tribes scattered among the nations." The Dispersion means those Jewish Christians who had been "dispersed" (scattered) away from Israel. Although James' original audience were mainly from a Jewish background, the inclusion of his circular letter in the Bible shows that it has much to say to all Christians.

How does he describe his readers in chapter 1? (See verses 2, 16 and 19.)

"My brothers" (v 2). "My beloved brothers" (v 16, 19).

It will be helpful to keep this in mind as we read parts of James' letter. Even when he has some very hard things to say, he is writing to "beloved" fellow Christians, both male and female (the plural "brothers" regularly refers to both men and women).

Speak truth in love + humility

▶ **WATCH DVD 5.1** (7 min 11 sec) **OR DELIVER TALK 5.1** (see page 106)

* *Encourage the group to make notes as they watch the DVD or listen to the talk. There is space for notes on page 95 of the Handbook.*

👉 **JAMES 2:1-10**

¹ My brothers, show no partiality as you hold the faith in our Lord Jesus Christ, the Lord of glory. ² For if a man wearing a gold ring and fine cloth-ing comes into your assembly, and a poor man in shabby clothing also comes in, ³ and if you pay attention to the one who wears the fine cloth-ing and say, "You sit here in a good place," while you say to the poor man, "You stand over there," or, "Sit down at my feet," ⁴ have you not then made distinctions among yourselves and become judges with evil thoughts? ⁵ Listen, my beloved brothers, has not God chosen those who are poor in the world to be rich in faith and heirs of the kingdom, which he has promised to those who love him? ⁶ But you have dishonored the poor man. Are not the rich the ones who oppress you, and the ones who drag you into court? ⁷ Are they not the ones who blaspheme the honorable name by which you were called?

⁸ If you really fulfill the royal law according to the Scripture, "You shall love your neighbor as yourself," you are doing well. ⁹ But if you show partiality, you are committing sin and are convicted by the law as transgressors. ¹⁰ For whoever keeps the whole law but fails in one point has become account-able for all of it.

NOTE: A revision of the ESV in August 2016, brought out after Stephen Um was filmed but before this book was printed, has changed James 2:10 to say, *"For whoever keeps the whole law but fails in one point has become **guilty of** all of it."*

Discuss

Do you agree that money is "the elephant in the room" (or, perhaps, "the elephant in the church"!)? Why do you think that is?

The phrase "the elephant in the room" is used of a big issue that everyone is aware of but nobody wants to talk about. Reasons people may give for not wanting to talk about money include: "It's private," "I'm ashamed of how much / how little I earn," "I don't want to be judged," "I'm worried I'll be told to give it all away." Of course, your group may disagree that money is "the elephant in the room." If so, the rest of these discussion questions may be easy for you!

 JAMES 1:9-11

⁹ Let the lowly brother boast in his exaltation, ¹⁰ and the rich in his humiliation, because like a flower of the grass he will pass away. ¹¹ For the sun rises with its scorching heat and withers the grass; its flower falls, and its beauty perish-es. So also will the rich man fade away in the midst of his pursuits.

What do we learn about the rich in these verses?

- v 10: Christians who are financially rich should boast in their low position as believers (i.e. that their faith is a gift from God, not something they have earned).
- v 11: Money is temporary. Like a flower in full bloom, the rich person may look beautiful and perfect, but since his riches don't last, he too fades away.

JAMES 1:16-18

16 Do not be deceived, my beloved brothers. 17 Every good gift and every perfect gift is from above, coming down from the Father of lights, with whom there is no variation or shadow due to change. 18 Of his own will he brought us forth by the word of truth, that we should be a kind of firstfruits of his creatures.

What do verses 16-18 tell us about God?

- Every gift comes from him.
- His gifts are good and perfect.
- He is "the Father of lights" (ESV). (NIV says "Father of the heavenly lights.") God is the Creator of all, including all the planets and stars (Psalm 136:7-9).
- God doesn't change. Although God made the heavenly lights, he is not like them. We and they move, creating shadows that shift and change. God does not. He is constant, unchanging, and always good to us.
- He has given us new birth through "the word of truth," the gospel message.

Bearing in mind what God is like, let's think about money. If our money is a gift from God (v 17), how does that make you feel about a) your money, b) the things you have bought with your money, c) the ways you could spend your money?

a) Our money is ultimately given to us by God; it's not something we have earned or deserve (even if we have worked hard for it!). We should be thankful for the money God has given us, whether we have a lot or a little, and hold it loosely as something that still belongs to him.

b) The things we have bought, be they possessions, holidays or education, are also gifts from God. As with money, we should thank God for his immense generosity to us, and be looking for opportunities to use these things to serve him.

c) On the DVD, Stephen Um says, "Because money is a gift from God, we do not ultimately have the right to decide what is done with it." Ask your group if they agree with this view? Why / why not? What is the "risk" in agreeing that God is the one who has the right to decide how our money is used?

▶ **WATCH DVD 5.2** (7 min 37 sec) **OR DELIVER TALK 5.2** (see page 106)

* *Encourage the group to make notes as they watch the DVD or listen to the talk. There is space for notes on page 97 of the Handbook.*

👉 **JAMES 5:1-6**

¹ Come now, you rich, weep and howl for the miseries that are coming upon you. ² Your riches have rotted and your garments are moth-eaten. ³ Your gold and silver have corroded, and their corrosion will be evidence against you and will eat your flesh like fire. You have laid up treasure in the last days. ⁴ Behold, the wages of the laborers who mowed your fields, which you kept back by fraud, are crying out against you, and the cries of the harvesters have reached the ears of the Lord of hosts. ⁵ You have lived on the earth in luxury and in self-indulgence. You have fattened your hearts in a day of slaughter. ⁶ You have condemned and murdered the righteous person. He does not resist you.

Discuss

What does James accuse these rich people of doing?

* v 3: They have "laid up treasure" (ESV) / "hoarded wealth" (NIV).
* v 4: They have not paid their workers what they owed.
* v 5: They have lived in luxury and self-indulgence, and "fattened [their] hearts."
* v 6: They have "condemned and murdered the righteous person"—if not directly, then by allowing the poor to suffer and even die as a result of their actions or inaction.

It's easy to assume that we would never do these things, but what are the heart attitudes behind their actions?

- **Hoarding** (v 3): the heart attitudes include greed, self-importance, and maybe a lack of trust in God's provision.
- Fraud/injustice (v 4): the heart attitudes include self-centeredness, and putting our own desires ahead of others' needs.
- Self-indulgence (v 5): the heart attitudes include focusing on what we want now, rather than looking ahead to our future with Christ.
- Condemning the poor (v 6): the heart attitudes include selfishness, lack of care for those in need, and not bothering to check the impact of our actions.

It is very easy for us to treat wealth in an ungodly way. As you think about your money and possessions, when might you be tempted to show similar wrong attitudes in your heart?

The answers to this question will be personal to each member of your group, but may include some of the following: always upgrading to the latest phone/gadget to keep up with others; not checking whether the companies we support through our purchases treat their employees rightly (including the ones working in far-off countries); envying those who have more than us; not giving generously to those in need because we worry we may need more for ourselves in the future. (Note: There is a balance here. It may well be right to build some savings so that we are not a burden to others, but we easily fall into the trap of simply accumulating wealth rather than using it for good.)

▶ **WATCH DVD 5.3** (4 min 13 sec) **OR DELIVER TALK 5.3** (see page 106)

- *Encourage the group to make notes as they watch the DVD or listen to the talk. There is space for notes on page 99 of the Handbook.*

Discuss

"God does not hoard his riches—he freely gives them away. God does not defraud—he goes above and beyond and gives his very self. God is not self-indulgent—in the gospel he engages in self-deprivation for the good of others."

Think about any tendency you may have to be a hoarder or compulsive consumer. How will God's example help you to change?

Encourage the group to think about God's generous goodness. As his image-bearers (see Session 1, page 36-37) we are to reflect God's generosity to others.

Our motivation isn't simply that we *should* give generously, but that we have this *opportunity* to show God's generous nature to others, and to bring him glory.

Instead of being tempted toward fraud/injustice, how can you make God's giving of himself a pattern to follow for your own giving, even to the point where it hurts?

Again, God's character is our starting point. We have seen in Session 2 that God is a God of justice. So we will want to reflect that justice in how we treat others. Ask your group if they can think of ways in which they can hinder the poor from receiving all they should (even if these ways would not legally be considered "fraud"). For example, in the US many servers in restaurants are paid much less than the minimum wage on the expectation that the shortfall will be made up of tips. What does that mean for us as Christians when we decide whether and how much to tip?

"Self-indulgence is counter to our identity in Christ." How will the self-deprivation of Jesus help you to fight the temptation in your own heart to indulge yourself?

Jesus gave up all the riches of heaven to come to earth as our Savior (Philippians 2:5-8). He then suffered and died a horrific death so that we could be offered the free gift of eternal life. Reminding ourselves of these things, and looking ahead to being with Christ in the new creation, will help us fight the temptations of our own hearts.

What are you going to change as a result of this session?

Give people a few minutes to write down any changes they want to make in their own lives. Ask those who can to tell the rest of the group one thing they have written down, so that you can all pray for one another this week.

Pray

Look again at your list of God's characteristics on page 97. Taking each one in turn, thank him for this aspect of his goodness and ask him to help you live as his image-bearers.

DAILY BIBLE DEVOTIONALS

Jesus' teaching on money is powerful, uncompromising and uncomfortable to modern ears. But each of the six passages we look at in the daily devotionals packs a punch that we need to listen to if we are to be faithful followers of Christ.

SERMONS

OPTION ONE: JAMES 2:1-10

This is one of the passages Stephen uses in his DVD presentation, which could be expanded upon in a sermon.

OPTION TWO: 2 CORINTHIANS 8:1-15

The Bible study is based on the second half of this passage (see next page), and it could be expanded upon in a sermon.

OPTION THREE: LUKE 12:16-21

This passage is not mentioned in this material, but it reveals the Lord's attitude toward money and its dangers—how it can rob us of eternal life.
- The idea that our possessions define us is not new.
- The man in Jesus' story mistook his wealth for God's approval; and mistook time for eternity.
- We are fools if we make the same mistake.

If one of your Sunday sermons is to be based on the theme of this session, church members will find a page to write notes on the sermon on page 111 of their Handbooks.

Luke 12:13-21

James 2:1-10

2 Corinthians 8:1-15

New York Times → Idolatry + Wealth

BIBLE STUDY

AIM: In the main session, we reflected on how uncomfortable we are about thinking and talking openly about money. We know that generosity is part of our gospel response, but our temptation is to "tame" it into culturally acceptable ways.

Discuss

When someone talks about money, giving or special collections, what are some reactions that go on inside our heads? Why?

You might like to put some positives and negatives on a flip chart or sheet of paper for this. There are lots of potential negative or erroneous answers: "Not again!"; "How can I afford more?"; "I'm not sure that is an important thing to give money to"; "I'm not sure that this money is being spent well"; "This church is greedy"; "I need to give so that God will bless me"; "God will give me a double blessing as I give today."

Positives might include: "This is a great thing to give to"; "I would love to support this ministry"; "This would be worthwhile to give extra to"; "God has blessed me richly so I will make a thank offering for this."

Many of the reactions we naturally have are focused on justifying our own lack of willingness to give, or on the wisdom or trustworthiness of the church to administer and spend wisely.

👉 READ 2 CORINTHIANS 8:1-15

¹ We want you to know, brothers, about the grace of God that has been given among the churches of Macedonia, ² for in a severe test of affliction, their abundance of joy and their extreme poverty have overflowed in a wealth of generosity on their part. ³ For they gave according to their means, as I can testify, and beyond their means, of their own accord...

1. What is remarkable about the giving of the Macedonian churches?

- They were severely afflicted (v 2).
- They were joyful.
- They were extremely poor.
- Yet they gave generously within their means… (v 3)
- … and even beyond them (v 3). Tease out what this might mean. Some definitions might be: they gave in a way that hurt their own lifestyle, or required them to cancel or delay some of their personal plans and hopes, or else they gave in a way that a "sensible" friend or family member would think was ridiculous.

Where does this come from? How is it described?

It is described as a "grace"—it comes from God (v 1), and is supernatural. Grace is God's undeserved kindness to them in saving them through Jesus. This group of Christians were so overwhelmed by the generosity of God toward them that they were moved to give generously to others.

2. How did the Macedonians view their giving?

- *It was a privilege (v 4).* They were thankful to God for the opportunity to help their brothers and sisters in need.
- *It was a natural part of their discipleship (v 5).* It was simply an aspect of their giving themselves to the Lord. This is an important principal: generosity and giving is not a "bolt-on extra" to the Christian life; it is integral to it.

How is this attitude toward giving in conflict with our culture's view of wealth?

Our culture's view of money is that it is ours to keep, and dispose of as we wish. We are encouraged to save, to make wise plans and to take care of ourselves and our own before we consider giving to others. If we had experienced a severe affliction, we would be justifying spending out on a holiday for ourselves to recuperate. Instead the Macedonians just give and keep giving—joyfully.

Of course, we are also called to manage our money well and prudently—to provide for our families and not live in debt. But planning how we use God's gift of wealth must not squash a basic instinct to be generous and sacrificial.

3. How is this a challenge to the Corinthian church (v 7)?

These poor Christians gave with enormous generosity. And yet the wealthy Corinthians need to be urged and encouraged to give. The Corinthian church took great pride in their "spiritual excellence" in the areas of faith, knowledge, and speech. Paul urges them to seek excellence in the grace of generosity also. He is suggesting that their "excellence" is really not worth that much at all if it does not extend to generosity; that their focus on "excellence" may be a mask for self serving and lack of love.

In what ways might we have a similar attitude to the Corinthians?

Spend some time on this. Our churches can easily look down on the Corinthians for their lack of love, party spirit, and enthusiastic but empty worship. And yet, here the problem is that though they had great faith, were good at preaching and talking, and knew a lot (v 7), their spiritual poverty was revealed by their lack of generosity.

4. Does Paul command them to give? What motive is he looking for (v 7-9)?

- He does not command it, but challenges them to show that their love is genuine by this act of grace in giving generously to those in severe need (v 8). This opportunity is a God-given test of their sincerity.
- Giving to help other Christians in need is about far more than doing the right thing or being a good witness. It's a matter of whether we truly love Jesus and his people, and humans created by God.
- Jesus is the ultimate example and pattern. We are saved because he gave up the riches of heaven to die in poverty for us. His spiritual poverty has made us spiritually rich.

What makes a gift "acceptable" (v 9-14)? How will that involve our head (what we think), our heart (what we feel), and our hands (what we do)?

Paul sees that head, heart and hands need to be connected to make a gift acceptable.
- Head: the motive should be to honor Christ.
- Heart: they must "desire to do it."
- Hands: they must give (and follow through on it, v 11).

It is nothing to do with the size of the gift, but rather the need, and controversially, fairness. There is clearly an element of justice about this—Paul is calling for "fairness," which implies the redistribution of wealth. Some of the group may be uncomfortable with this thought if it conflicts with their political instincts. If the group starts to argue, get them to focus on the Bible verse and ask what it means and does not mean.

5. What does the picture in verse 15 add to our understanding of generosity?

It springs from a deep trust in God's promise to be our provider. It is also an example of the principle of "fairness" playing out. Each had sufficient for themselves.
- True generosity must trust God for provision.
- The reference is to the gathering of manna by God's people in the wilderness. They had to gather just enough for a single day, and everyone had sufficient for their needs (Exodus 16:18).
- When there is a need, we are being encouraged to ignore the worldly prudence that governs much of our thinking about money, and give generously, trusting that God will supply our need.
- The principle could be summed up as: "If I have what I need (not what I want), and another person does not, then I should give to them, so that there might be equality."

Apply

FOR YOURSELF: How does the giving described here compare with your own thinking about money and giving?

Refer back to the answers you gave in Question 1. Compare with the following:
- Their giving wasn't hindered by severe trials or extreme poverty (v 2).
- It was accompanied by overflowing joy (v 2).
- They gave as much as they were able to, and even beyond (v 3).
- They took the initiative in giving (v 3).
- They viewed it as a privilege and begged to do it (v 4).
- They exceeded Paul's expectations in their giving (v 5).
- Their giving flowed out of their relationship with the Lord—seeing themselves in submission to and service of him. In other words, it was part of their worship (v 5).

Pray

FOR YOURSELF: Ask God to give you "the grace of giving" as you reflect on the Lord Jesus who gave up "sapphire-paved courts for stable floor." Pray that you would be eager, willing and practical in your approach to giving in the future.

FOR YOUR CHURCH: Ask God to make you generous like your Macedonian brothers and sisters of old.

FURTHER READING

> *You can always give without loving, but you can never love without giving.*
> **Amy Carmichael**

> *If you have money, power, and status today, it is due to the century and place in which you were born, to your talents and capacities and health, none of which you earned. In short, all your resources are in the end the gift of God.*
> **Tim Keller**

> *If our charities do not at all pinch or hamper us, I should say they are too small. There ought to be things we should like to do and cannot do because our charitable expenditure excludes them.*
> **C. S. Lewis**

Books

- *His Mission: Jesus in the Gospel of Luke*, chapter 6 "Jesus and Money" (Stephen Um)
- *Sex and Money* (Paul David Tripp)
- *Health, Wealth & Happiness: Has the Prosperity Gospel Overshadowed the Gospel of Christ?* (David W. Jones and Russell S. Woodbridge)
- *Living in the Light: Money, Sex and Power* (John Piper)
- *Money Counts* (Graham Beynon)
- *James For You* (Sam Allberry)

Online

- *Obligation, Stewardship, and the Poor:* gospelshapedchurch.org/resources551
- *9 Marks of a Generous Giver:* gospelshapedchurch.org/resources552
- *How the Gospel Makes Us Generous and Content with Our Money:* gospelshapedchurch.org/resources553
- *Generosity (Theology Refresh: Podcast for Christian Leaders) (video):* gospelshapedchurch.org/resources554
- *How to Identify and Redeem Your "Money Motivators":* gospelshapedchurch.org/resources555

LEADER'S REFLECTIONS

SESSION 6:

RECONCILIATION: RELATIONSHIPS HEALED

PART OF LIVING IN A WORLD THIS SIDE OF SHALOM IS THE REALITY OF BROKEN RELATIONSHIPS. THE FRIEND WE'VE GIVEN THE COLD SHOULDER TO; THE FAMILY MEMBER WE HARBOR A BITTERNESS AGAINST; THE ARGUMENT OVER WHICH WE'VE NEVER MADE UP. IS THERE ANY HOPE FOR OUR RELATIONAL MESSES? THIS SESSION, WE'LL FOCUS IN ON JUST ONE WORD: RECONCILIATION.

TALK OUTLINE

6.1 • Reconciliation is "reuniting; bringing back together." But it isn't only a thing for far-off political issues or "tragic cases"—it is **local** and **personal** to all of us.

6.2 • **EVERYONE NEEDS RECONCILIATION** *Matthew 5:21-26*
  - Jesus' interpretation of the law raises the moral stakes. Anger = murder (v 21-22). Insults lead to judgment (v 22).
  - Jesus takes unreconciled relationships very seriously. The first step to reconciliation is understanding that we need it—we are not innocent.

• **EVERYONE IS RESPONSIBLE FOR RECONCILIATION**
Seeking reconciliation is your responsibility (v 23-24). It's not just for specialists. The man in the illustration must leave his gift at the altar and seek reconciliation. This sounds costly, dangerous and humiliating—but it is essential.

• **THE IMPORTANCE OF RECONCILIATION**
  - We can't separate our **vertical relationship** with God from our **horizontal relationships** with others.
  - We rarely seek reconciliation with others because it is costly! It means we have to own our mess and make the first move.
  - We must admit that we're not the heroes in the story. Jesus shows us that we're just as much villains as anyone else. *We* are the tragic cases.
  - This is **urgent** (v 25-26). Take care of it quickly. It's your move.

6.3 • **THERE IS HOPE FOR THE UNRECONCILED** *Colossians 1:19-20*
  - Jesus left the glory of heaven and put himself in the midst of our chaos. **He came for tragic cases.** He came to set things right with people who set things wrong.
  - God did not *need* to be reconciled and was not *obliged* to be reconciled with us. Yet he took the full weight of responsibility on himself.
  - On the cross Jesus took all of our hatred, anger, envy, strife, resentment, bitterness and jealousy on himself and reconciled us to God forever.
  - Reconciliation is first and foremost something you receive—and then you re-gift it to others. **Pursue ordinary, everyday reconciliation.**

You can download a full transcript of these talks at
WWW.GOSPELSHAPEDCHURCH.ORG/MERCY/TALKS

RECONCILIATION: RELATIONSHIPS HEALED

NOTE: In this session we'll be looking at the issue of reconciliation. This is an important topic since the gospel of reconciliation, if seen worked out in our lives, is one way in which Christians can shine particularly brightly among non-believers. However, it may be a current and difficult issue for some in your group. It would be good to think in advance about how you (or someone from your church family) can offer support to anyone who is particularly struggling as a result of a lack of reconciliation, and who needs more help than it is possible (or appropriate) to give during the group session.

Discuss

How would you define "reconciliation," using a maximum of six words?

You may want to ask group members to have a go at this by themselves first before then comparing answers. You're not looking for a single "correct" definition—just using this as a way of introducing the topic. Possible answers might include: "bringing back together after break-up," "replacing war with peace," "restoration of friendship" or "reuniting those who have been separated."

▶ **WATCH DVD 6.1** (3 min 35 sec) **OR DELIVER TALK 6.1** (see page 126)

* *Encourage the group to make notes as they watch the DVD or listen to the talk. There is space for notes on page 115 of the Handbook.*

Discuss

This session is based on some of Jesus' teaching from the Sermon on the Mount (Matthew 5 – 7). Who was Jesus teaching? (See Matthew 5:1-2.) But who else was listening? (See Matthew 7:28-29.)

- Jesus was teaching his disciples (5:1), his closest followers. The Sermon on the Mount is teaching *Christians* how to live in a way that honors Christ.
- The wider crowds were listening (7:28). They were astonished at the authority with which Jesus was teaching, since this wasn't how the religious leaders of the day taught (7:29).

What are we to do with Jesus' teaching in the Sermon on the Mount? Read Matthew 7:24 and compare with 7:26.

We are not only to *listen* to Jesus' words, but also to *do* what he says. In other words, we are to be like the wise man, not like the foolish man.

Encourage your group to keep this in mind as you read and discuss today's main passage. It will raise issues that some will find hard, but we need to *listen* to what Jesus is saying and be ready (and eager!) to *do* what he says.

 MATTHEW 5:21-26

21 You have heard that it was said to those of old, "You shall not murder; and whoever murders will be liable to judgment." 22 But I say to you that every-one who is angry with his brother will be liable to judgment; whoever insults his brother will be liable to the council; and whoever says, "You fool!" will be liable to the hell of fire. 23 So if you are offering your gift at the altar and there remember that your brother has something against you, 24 leave your gift there before the altar and go. First be reconciled to your brother, and then come and offer your gift. 25 Come to terms quickly with your accuser while you are going with him to court, lest your accuser hand you over to the judge, and the judge to the guard, and you be put in prison. 26 Truly, I say to you, you will never get out until you have paid the last penny.

▶ **WATCH DVD 6.2** (11 min 49 sec) **OR DELIVER TALK 6.2** (see page 126)

- *Encourage the group to make notes as they watch the DVD or listen to the talk. There is space for notes on page 117 of the Handbook.*

Discuss

The sixth of the Ten Commandments says, "You shall not murder" (Exodus 20:13). In Matthew 5:22, what does Jesus say is the equivalent to murder?

Anger; insults; calling someone a fool.

At first glance, it could look as if Jesus lists these examples so that, as long as we avoid all of them, we can be sure we don't accidentally break the sixth commandment. But what deeper heart issue is Jesus revealing here?

The sixth commandment is about more than just the physical act of murder—it is about an attitude of the heart. When we hate someone else and want to hurt them, we are displaying part of the same heart condition that can lead to murder. The heart issue is hatred—effectively saying to someone, "I wish you didn't exist." And *all* of us react that way to others at times.

Jesus is revealing that we cannot keep even this single commandment (one that on the face of it looks easy to keep). As Stephen says in the DVD: "His teaching here is not primarily about what we need to *do*, but about our utter need for a Savior."

Reconciliation is at the heart of the Christian faith, as shown by our need for a Savior who can reconcile us to God. Jesus speaks, here, about the need to be reconciled with our fellow Christians. How do we know from these verses that this kind of reconciliation is important to God? Why do you think this is?

Verse 24 tells us that we are to "leave [our] gift … and go." We know that reconciliation is important to God because we are told to deal with it *before* we finish making our offering to him. The modern equivalent would be to leave a church service before the end in order to find your Christian brother or sister and be reconciled with them.

Reconciliation is central to the gospel. It is only because of the sacrificial death and resurrection of Christ that we can be forgiven for all our sinfulness (including all the ways we break the sixth commandment) and brought back into a right relationship with God. Our reconciliation with others, imperfect thought it may be, is a picture of the perfect reconciliation we have with God through Christ.

In these verses, we see that failing to seek reconciliation is the equivalent of murder in the eyes of God. What does Jesus say we are to do if/when we remember that we are not reconciled with someone else? Are these instructions for all Christians, or for those God has especially chosen to be peacemakers?

- Verse 24—Leave what we are doing (even if it's an act of worship) and go to the person concerned.
- Verse 24—Do whatever we need to in order to be reconciled. While it may turn out that our brother/sister is unwilling to be reconciled with us, we must do whatever we can to make it possible. (Note: If the other person is unwilling for things to be put right, but we have done all we can to address our own anger toward them, we are no longer guilty of the equivalent of murder, v 22.)
- Verse 25—Do it quickly.

Jesus' teaching is for "everyone" (v 22). This is a command that we are all to listen to and obey (like the wise man in Matthew 7:24).

NOTE: Some in your group may know that the Sermon on the Mount does directly address "peacemakers" in Matthew 5:9. These "Beatitudes" are a list of blessings that are for all Christians. It's not that some are to be meek (v 5), some to be merciful (v 7), some to be peacemakers (v 9), etc. We are all called to reflect all of these attitudes.

▶ **WATCH DVD 6.3** (5 min 57 sec) **OR DELIVER TALK 6.3** (see page 126)

- *Encourage the group to make notes as they watch the DVD or listen to the talk. There is space for notes on page 118 of the Handbook.*

👉 **COLOSSIANS 1:19-20**

> ¹⁹ *For in him all the fullness of God was pleased to dwell, ²⁰ and through him to reconcile to himself all things, whether on earth or in heaven, making peace by the blood of his cross.*

Discuss

"The practice of reconciliation is simply the act of re-gifting what you have received to someone else." Think about the following scenarios. How could you, either as individuals or as a church family, "re-gift" the reconciliation you have received in these situations?

NOTE: These scenarios move from an easier, less personal example to those that may well be closer to home for your own church family. If you are short of time, you may want to focus just on the third example, as this is the one that addresses issues of church unity.

- **As you are dropping your child at school, you see two mothers having an argument. How could you act as a peacemaker in this situation?**

The temptation is to keep clear, either pretending the argument isn't happening or just watching from a distance. But God didn't "keep clear" from us. As Stephen Um said, *"God, the Judge of all humankind, was not obliged to act in reconciliation. He could have left us to face the consequences of our rebellion against him. Here is the greatest mystery of God's love for us: the one who had no need for reconciliation took the full responsibility for it upon himself."* So, if we want to reflect God's attitude to us—to "re-gift" the reconciliation we have received—we will want to step in and try and help these mothers to make peace. Initially, this may mean going up to them and joining the conversation, trying to calm the emotions. Then maybe invite both mothers to join you for a coffee so that you can all talk about the cause of the argument and see if it can be calmly resolved.

- **In the last year, a couple have left your church because they were unhappy with the style of music. What would it look like to reach out to them—not necessarily to try and bring them back into your church family, but to be reconciled with them?**

Again, the temptation is to leave things as they are, especially since you no longer see this couple every Sunday. But harsh or unwise things may have been said in the build-up to them leaving. Talk about who would be the best person/group to contact this couple, and how to do that. What could you say or do to address any ill-feeling? Would it help to meet up with them, or to invite them to join you for a meal or coffee? How can you keep Christ at the center of your reconciliation, rather than any debate about music styles?

NOTE: Occasionally, circumstances can mean it is right for someone to move from one church to another, even if they are not leaving the neighborhood. You may want to discuss what it would look like for someone to "leave well" rather than there being misunderstanding or anger about them leaving.

- **A long-standing member of your church family has recently died. At the funeral, her two sons, also church members, start arguing over which of them** should inherit a valuable painting. How can you help them to be reconciled?

It may seem that a funeral isn't the right time to "interfere," but this situation is quite like Jesus' example in Matthew 5. The reconciliation of these two sons matters to God and should be addressed quickly. Since this family are all members of the church, it would be good to remind them that the funeral of a Christian is an opportunity to thank God that this person is now rejoicing with him. This is only possible because of the reconciliation brought about by Christ. In the same way, these two sons need to be reconciled, and to be a godly witness to any non-Christians who knew their mother.

These scenarios were invented. But how can you apply your answers to them to current situations facing you, either as individuals or within the church?

Depending on both your group and your church, there may be one or more current situations that you can discuss at this point. Alternatively, give members of the group some time to think quietly about any personal situations that require reconciliation and/or to pray for others who have experienced some kind of breakdown of relationship.

Pray

"Jesus opened up the cosmic filing cabinet, pulled out our record of law-breaking, and replaced it with his perfect record of law-keeping."

Spend some time praising and thanking Jesus for making it possible for us to be reconciled to God through his death and resurrection.

Think about anyone with whom you need to be reconciled. Confess to God your part in the breakdown of that relationship. Ask him to help you to obey Jesus' words by going to that person and doing whatever rightly needs to be done to be reconciled with them.

Pray for those you know who have a wider role as peacemakers—maybe your church leaders, those working in the local community, or those in wider government. Ask God to give them wisdom and grace as they seek to bring people back together.

DAILY BIBLE DEVOTIONALS

This week's daily Bible devotionals pick up both the challenge and opportunity involved in Jesus' call for us to be peacemakers. Our model for reconciliation comes from the gospel, in which we are reconciled to God and one another through Christ. Everything flows from this...

SERMONS

👉 **OPTION ONE: MATTHEW 5:21-26**

This passage is the one Stephen focuses on in the main session, which could be expanded upon in a sermon (you might choose to look at the whole of chapter 5).

👉 **OPTION TWO: PHILIPPIANS 4:2-7**

This is the passage the Bible study is based on (see next page), which could also be expanded upon in a sermon.

👉 **OPTION THREE: MATTHEW 18:15**

This passage is not mentioned in this material, but it paints a beautiful picture of reconciliation:
- Jesus describes an escalating process for dealing with relational issues and personal sin. But we want to focus less on the process than on the hope in v 15.
- When someone has done something wrong, approach them privately, gently and humbly to talk about it. Make repentance easy for them, not hard.
- The aim in this is to "[gain] your brother"—to help them be united with you and the Lord, not to set yourself up against them or judge them.

If one of your Sunday sermons is to be based on the theme of this session, church members will find a page to write notes on the sermon on page 131 of their Handbooks.

BIBLE STUDY

AIM: The aim of reconciliation is to establish peace—*shalom*—between two people, families, communities or nations at war with each other. And *shalom* is the environment in which we flourish as human beings. But how do we strive for *shalom* now, when so many of our relationships are strained or fractured? In this study we'll see from Philippians how to help bring reconciliation to others in our church community and beyond.

Discuss

Think of a time when you were in need of reconciliation with someone else. What happened? How was the situation resolved? What was it that kept you apart for so long?

> Invite a couple of group members to share their stories—but encourage them to sum it up in a few sentences. This may be funny, or extremely painful. Group members may have ongoing situations that are very uncomfortable for them. It will be worth reminding the group that what God calls us to can be both difficult and costly. The word of God addresses real life in all its hurt and pain. Reassure them that the group is a "safe place" to talk about these things, and that members will not gossip, but be prayerful for them if this is a deeply troubling issue for them. It will be important to prepare your own example in case no one is willing to share theirs.

 READ PHILIPPIANS 4:2-7

> ² *I entreat Euodia and I entreat Syntyche to agree in the Lord.* ³ *Yes, I ask you also, true companion, help these women, who have labored side by side with me in the gospel together with Clement and the rest of my fellow workers, whose names are in the book of life.*

1. **What encouraging things do verses 2-3 tell us about the two women Euodia and Syntyche?**

- They are both Christians.
- They labored at Paul's side—they worked with Paul to tell others the gospel (see 1:27).
- Paul considered them to be his "fellow workers."
- Their names are in "the book of life." Explain that this phrase means that they are Christians, and that because they have put their faith in Jesus, they can be certain of having eternal life (see Revelation 20:15; 21:27).

We don't know the details of their disagreement. Why do you think Paul steers clear of the nature of their disagreement?

Their disagreement cannot have been about false teaching which threatened the gospel. If it had been, we can be sure that Paul would have corrected that false teaching just as he had done in chapter 3. Perhaps the most important point is that, when people become hostile towards each other, they start to make a record of wrongs, and every perceived insult or misunderstanding becomes a reason for staying hostile. In this situation, getting to grips with details can be counterproductive.

Instead, Paul points to their common identity in Christ, and their partnership together and with him in gospel mission.

2. What does it mean to "agree in the Lord" (v 2-3)?

We must remember that we are united in Christ, have the same heavenly Father, and should have the same purpose—to know Christ and to make him known.

We may disagree on the precise way to understand some parts of the Bible, or on how we do things as Christians, but we must not let these things ruin our unity on the important things. It is understandable that Christians will disagree with each other in all kinds of things, but we must agree about the thing that unites us—Christ and the gospel. Not only that, we must also let the main things be the main things—Euodia and Syntyche are to act out of gospel unity and friendship, and see other problems as details, rather than acting out of their disagreement and seeing their gospel unity as a mere detail.

Why is Paul so anxious for them to agree with each other (see also 2:3-5; 1:27)?

- In 2:3-5 Paul has already said that Christians are to "count others more significant than yourselves" and that their "attitude is to be the same as that of Christ Jesus" (NIV). Both women need to be prepared to adopt the attitude of Jesus—taking the initiative, making themselves humble and serving others—even if such actions come at a great personal cost.
- In 1:27 Paul says, "Let your manner of life be worthy of the gospel of Christ." In this way they will be "standing firm in one spirit, with one mind striving side by side for the faith of the gospel."
- If these women are going to show the same attitude as Christ, they need to agree in the Lord. If they don't, their conduct will have an impact on how they and the rest of the Philippian Christians share the gospel with unbelievers.

3. How can others be involved in helping their brothers and sisters to be reconciled (4:2-3)?

- Paul did not take sides. There may be things to apologize for, but the bigger problem is the lack of reconciliation—not necessarily the things that caused it. Instead we should aim to help those who disagree to be reconciled.
- The problem is not just for the women. It is a problem for the whole congregation—that's why Paul appeals for congregation members to be part of the reconciliation process.
- We should remind each other of the things that unite us: who Jesus is, why he came and our responsibility to tell others about him.
- See also 2:1-4: we must have the same love, be in full accord and of one mind, and do nothing from rivalry or conceit. There may be things that we need to repent of in our disagreements.

4. What clues are there in verses 4-7 about how we can be maintainers of peace, as well as makers of it?

- *Joy (v 4):* Division often arises from discontent in some form or other. When we are joyful—recognizing what we have received from God in the gospel—we will radiate a contentment that others will be hungry for, and we will show that our priorities are in a positive place.
- *Reasonableness (v 5):* Some have joked that Euodia and Syntyche might be

called "Odious and Soon-touchy." When we react unreasonably to others, or let our emotions get out of proportion, we can easily drive others away from us and create difficult situations. Having a sense of perspective and a willingness to ponder things away from our immediate emotional reaction will help stop conflict from developing.

- *Understand the times (v 5):* "The Lord is at hand"; Jesus is both present with us, and will also return to judge. We are in the era of gospel witness to the world, and that needs to be our chief goal and focus. Anything that slows, distracts or deflects us from that must be done away with.
- *Prayer (v 6):* When we are angry with someone else, we should pray for them, and for our own reaction to them. This will help us respond better and love them more. And God will answer our prayers for these problems. He does that!
- *Thanksgiving (v 6):* When we are grateful, we are content. When we are able to thank the Lord for the people we struggle with relationally, it helps us to think about them differently.
- *Dependence on God (v 7):* This is a wonderful promise to claim if you are anxious about a relationship. But it is also an instruction to continue to dwell on the gospel and how it has changed you. God's peace, won for us through Jesus' death on the cross, is now what should control our hearts and minds— our emotional reactions to others, what we do in response to them, and how we think about them and the situation. We need to keep the work of Jesus as our constant reference point.

5. **Paul's advice is for Christians helping other Christians to reconcile. How might we help reconcile family, friends, work colleagues or people in our community who may not be believers?**

We cannot appeal to our unity in Christ, the commands of the gospel, or the importance of our witness when the parties are not believers. But there are ways in which we can point out the harm that people are doing to themselves and to others. Unforgiveness takes a terrible toll on those who hang on to it. There is always collateral damage in a family or community when people pursue a hostile or silent feud.

By being calm, rational and gentle, we may be able to point people away from focusing on the problem and help them look for solutions. We can also help them get out of unhelpful cycles of thought by asking good questions: "What would it take for you two to be brought together again?"; "No one is ever completely innocent in these things. What part do you think you might have played in getting this situation to where it is?" It may be that you can appeal to someone to "be the better man or woman" and take the initiative.

In the end, though, we need to recognize that our appeals may fall on deaf ears. Forgiveness is hard, as is admitting wrong. But Jesus says that peacemakers will be blessed (Matthew 5:9) , so it is important that we strive to play this role wherever we have the opportunity. Reconciliation can be an enormous blessing to families, workplaces and whole communities, to the benefit of all.

6. Think again about some of the situations you discussed or thought about in the opening question. What pieces of Paul's godly wisdom might have made the situation better?

Try to make this a practical answer. Be aware that nothing might have helped! In which case, the conclusion would be verse 7. Even when peace has proven impossible, we must still strive to make our own reactions to others come from the gospel of peace.

Apply

FOR YOURSELF: Choose one character trait of a "peacemaker" from question 4. How can you help yourself to grow in this?

FOR YOUR CHURCH: Are there any divisions between people or groups in your church, perhaps that have gone on for a long time? It is a problem for all of you. How will you pursue reconciliation as those whose names are "in the book of life" (v 3)?

IN YOUR NATION: How can you be a voice for reconciliation in your community or on a wider stage in your country? What is one positive step you can take to be part of the solution, and not the problem?

Pray

FOR YOUR CHURCH: Pray for any situations you have discussed where there is still no reconciliation. Pray especially that peacemakers and church leaders might take the initiative to restore people to love and fellowship with each other.

FOR THOSE YOU KNOW: Pray for marriages, parents and children, and whole families known to you where there is the pain of broken relationships. Pray for forgiveness, healing and hope.

FOR YOUR COMMUNITY: Pray for community leaders, politicians and national leaders—that they would seek peace and the common good, especially in places and countries where there are deep divisions and painful histories.

FURTHER READING

> God did not wait for a change of heart on our part. He made the first move. Indeed, he did more than that. He did all that was necessary to secure our reconciliation, including our change of heart.
>
> **Jerry Bridges**

> The gospel being what it is and always will be … our churches should be the most reconciling, peaceable, relaxed, happy places in town. We are so open to enemies, so meek in the face of insults and injuries, so forgiving toward the undeserving—if we do make people angry, let this be the reason. We refuse to join in their selfish battles. We're following a higher call. We are the peacemakers, the true sons of God.
>
> **Ray Ortland**

> He that is not a son of peace is not a son of God. All other sins destroy the church consequentially; but division and separation demolish it directly.
>
> **Richard Baxter**

Books

- *The Peacemaker: A Biblical Guide to Resolving Personal Conflict* (Ken Sande)
- *Resolving Everyday Conflict* (Ken Sande and Kevin Johnson)
- *The Peacemaking Pastor: A Biblical Guide to Resolving Church Conflict* (Alfred Poirier)

Online

- *How to Move from Forgiveness to Reconciliation:*
  gospelshapedchurch.org/resources561
- *That Part of Gospel-Centeredness We Avoid:*
  gospelshapedchurch.org/resources562
- *Four Things It's Okay to Say When You're Hurt:*
  gospelshapedchurch.org/resources563
- *Must We Forgive Those Who Sin Against Us If They Don't Repent?* (video)
  gospelshapedchurch.org/resources564

LEADER'S REFLECTIONS

SESSION 7:

DIVERSITY: COMMUNITY ENRICHED

FOR THE MOST PART, THE WESTERN WORLD IS NOW
ALLERGIC TO STATEMENTS, POLICIES, IDEOLOGIES AND
GROUPS THAT ARE ACTIVELY OPPOSED TO DIVERSITY.
BUT THERE'S A HUGE DIFFERENCE BETWEEN TALKING
ABOUT DIVERSITY AND ACTUALLY EMBRACING IT. AND
THAT'S A PROBLEM IN OUR CHURCHES TOO. TO HELP US,
WE'LL TAKE ANOTHER THRILLING LOOK AT WHERE OUR
GOSPEL COMMUNITIES ARE HEADING – TO GOD'S PERFECT
SHALOM-SHAPED NEW CREATION.

TALK OUTLINE

7.1 ● WHO IS MY NEIGHBOR? *Luke 10:25-37*

Most of us like the idea of "loving our neighbor." But like the lawyer in Luke 10, we tend to want to limit the scope to:

- **geographical neighbors:** our family and those on our street.
- **relational neighbors:** friends, co-workers, church members.

But Jesus' definition of "neighbor" puts the emphasis on the "other"—those with whom we are uncomfortable. To be faithful to Christ's radical vision of neighbor-love, we must not only talk about diversity but actively embrace it.

7.2 ● GOD'S INTENTION FOR DIVERSITY *Revelation 7:9-14*

- John sees a beautiful picture of diversity in Revelation 7: an assembly "no one could number," with every nation, tribe, people and language represented.
- In the new creation there is **unity in diversity**. Distinctives are not obliterated but celebrated—yet ultimate identity is found in wearing white robes of righteousness. The church must model this kind of unity in diversity.
- This sounds good, but there is a problem: **our inclination for uniformity**. We are drawn to people like ourselves. Martin Luther King said that Sunday morning is the most segregated hour in the nation! But when churches do realize the vision of unity in diversity, it is both beautiful and deeply countercultural.
- Unless we work intentionally to include people from other ethnicities, generations, and socio-economic groups, we will passively exclude them.

7.3 ● THE PROMISE OF UNITY IN DIVERSITY *Revelation 7:13-17*

- How can we become the kind of community that pleases God?
- Revelation shows us that **God wins**: he **will** bring about the *shalom* he desires. He will heal our wounds, wipe away our tears—and be the glue of our unity-in-diversity. Christ reconciles us to God, and shows us how to reconcile with others.
- **Be intentional:** Are you in significant warm relationships with those who are unlike you? Consider a practical first step. Start a conversation TODAY!
- **Be uncomfortable:** Embrace the fact that you will find this uncomfortable! The gospel drives us into unknown territory—but God is leading us toward the *shalom* he has ultimately purchased at the cost of Christ's blood.

You can download a full transcript of these talks at
WWW.GOSPELSHAPEDCHURCH.ORG/MERCY/TALKS

DIVERSITY: COMMUNITY ENRICHED

Discuss

This session is titled "Diversity: Community Enriched." Is your local community currently enriched by diversity? If so, how?

Apply this question initially to your local neighborhood. How diverse is it? How, if at all, does this diversity enrich the community? Then ask the same questions about your church family.

▶ **WATCH DVD 7.1** (6 min 1 sec) **OR DELIVER TALK 7.1** (see page 144)

* *Encourage the group to make notes as they watch the DVD or listen to the talk. There is space for notes on page 135 of the Handbook.*

☛ **LUKE 10:29-37**

29 But he, desiring to justify himself, said to Jesus, "And who is my neighbor?" 30 Jesus replied, "A man was going down from Jerusalem to Jericho, and he fell among robbers, who stripped him and beat him and departed, leaving him half dead. 31 Now by chance a priest was going down that road, and when he saw him he passed by on the other side. 32 So likewise a Levite, when he came to the place and saw him, passed by on the other side. 33 But a Samaritan, as he journeyed, came to where he was, and when he saw him, he had compassion. 34 He went to him and bound up his wounds, pouring on oil and wine. Then he set him on his own animal and brought him to an inn and took care of him. 35 And the next day he took out two denarii and gave them to the innkeeper, saying, 'Take care of him, and whatever more you spend, I will repay you when I come back.' 36 Which of these three, do you think, proved to be a neighbor to the man who fell among the robbers?"

37 He said, "The one who showed him mercy." And Jesus said to him, "You go, and do likewise."

Discuss

What question did the lawyer ask Jesus (verse 29)? How did he then answer his own question (verses 36-37)?

- Verse 29—the lawyer asked, "Who is my neighbor?"
- Verses 36-37—he told Jesus that the one who "proved to be a neighbor" was "the one who showed him mercy."

Jesus' parable doesn't tell us "who" our neighbor is so much as "how" to be a neighbor. How are we to be neighbors to others? How do we know from the parable that this applies to more than just those who live close to us?

- We are to be neighbors by "showing mercy," the very thing this whole curriculum has been about.
- In the parable, the man who showed mercy was a Samaritan—a non-Jew from a race hated and mistrusted by the Jews. (In contrast, the two people who passed by without helping were Jewish religious leaders—a priest and a Levite.) Like the Samaritan, we are to show mercy to all who need it, no matter who they are or where they are from.

☞ REVELATION 7:9-14

9 After this I looked, and behold, a great multitude that no one could number, from every nation, from all tribes and peoples and languages, standing before the throne and before the Lamb, clothed in white robes, with palm branches in their hands, 10 and crying out with a loud voice, "Salvation belongs to our God who sits on the throne, and to the Lamb!" 11 And all the angels were standing around the throne and around the elders and the four living creatures, and they fell on their faces before the throne and worshiped God, 12 saying, "Amen! Blessing and glory and wisdom and thanksgiving and honor and power and might be to our God forever and ever! Amen."

13 Then one of the elders addressed me, saying, "Who are these, clothed in white robes, and from where have they come?" 14 I said to him, "Sir, you know." And he said to me, "These are the ones coming out of the great tribulation. They have washed their robes and made them white in the blood of the Lamb.

▶ **WATCH DVD 7.2** (11 min 4 sec) **OR DELIVER TALK 7.2** (see page 144)

* *Encourage the group to make notes as they watch the DVD or listen to the talk. There is space for notes on page 137 of the Handbook.*

Discuss

In Revelation 7, John sees a huge crowd standing before God's throne. Where are they from (verse 9)? How does one of the elders describe these people (verse 14)?

* Verse 9—the crowd are from every nation, all tribes, all peoples and all languages. This means there are no people groups—not even one—that aren't going to be represented in the new creation.
* Verse 14—the people in the crowd have "come out of the great tribulation," meaning they were persecuted believers (a huge encouragement to the original readers of Revelation, many of whom were facing persecution). Their robes have been washed and made white by the blood of Jesus, the Lamb (meaning their sin has been forgiven and their hearts washed clean through the death and resurrection of Christ).

What does John's vision have to do with the issue of diversity?

It shows us that, when God's people are all together with him in the new creation, we will be as diverse as it is possible to be! We will come from every possible background, and yet we will be united through the blood of the Lamb, wearing the same white robes of righteousness. If this is the future we are looking forward to, we will want to model this "unity-in-diversity" in our churches now.

Use the following questions from Stephen Um's talk to ask yourselves how well your church family is modeling this "unity-in-diversity":

* **Who do you go to church with? Is it primarily people that look like you, and talk like you?**

- What is the ethnic makeup of your congregation in comparison to the ethnic makeup of your neighborhood?

- Are you cultivating friendships with people in your congregation who are unlike you—a different generation; a different socio-economic group; a different ethnicity?

- Who do you spend your time with during the week? Who are your closest friends? Are they those who look and act like you? Do you have close friends who are radically different than you?

Encourage people to be honest in their answers, both where they are pleased to see that they already do have some diverse friendships, as well as where they recognize a need to do more. Don't spend too much time discussing practical responses at this stage as you will be looking at that after watching the third part of the DVD.

▶ **WATCH DVD 7.3** (6 min 30 sec) **OR DELIVER TALK 7.3** (see page 144)

- *Encourage the group to make notes as they watch the DVD or listen to the talk. There is space for notes on page 138 of the Handbook.*

Discuss

"The book of Revelation gives us a picture of what happens when God makes the world right. It is ultimately a foretelling of God's inevitable victory. In the end, GOD WINS and brings about the holistic shalom that he desires. He wants unity-in-diversity in his people—and he is going to get it."

How do you respond to this statement, and why?

Possible responses may include being excited to see how things will be in the new creation; encouraged that God's victory is inevitable; looking forward to *shalom* being restored; and challenged that your own church family could be a closer match to this end-time vision.

Look again at your answers to the "unity-in-diversity" questions on p. 138. What practical steps can you take to open up relationships with those who are unlike you? Include at least one idea that you can put into practice in the next 24 hours.

Try to encourage every member of your group to choose at least one practical step that they can take individually in the next 24 hours, and one they can take in the next week. Ask if there are also things you can do as a group or as a church family. For example, does your church culture assume a fairly educated approach to learning, or a white attitude to singing?

Look back over your notes and journal from the previous sessions.

● **What are some of the things you have been challenged to do as an individual so that you reflect God's mercy to those around you?**

● **What are some of the changes you could make as a church family to model mercy and work toward *shalom* in your neighborhood?**

Many of these sessions ended with an encouragement to make some changes in how we live. Ask people to look up what they wrote at the time, as well as anything they may have written in their weekly journal section.

If you have time, ask the group how they have been getting on with living out some of the action points from earlier in the course.

Pray

 REVELATION 7:9-10

⁹ After this I looked, and behold, a great multitude that no one could number, from every nation, from all tribes and peoples and languages, standing before the throne and before the Lamb, clothed in white robes, with palm branches in their hands, ¹⁰ and crying out with a loud voice, "Salvation belongs to our God who sits on the throne, and to the Lamb!"

Thank the Lord that, because of Jesus, you can look forward to being part of the great multitude standing before the throne and praising him.

Look at some of the practical things you have written on this page. Pray that you will be able to put these into practice to reflect God's mercy and bring *shalom* to this world.

DAILY BIBLE DEVOTIONALS

The final set of devotionals looks at the history of diversity in the Bible. From creation and the dawn of diversity at the Tower of Babel, through the Old and New Testaments, to the glorious vision of God's diverse but united people worshiping before the throne of God in eternity.

SERMONS

👉 OPTION ONE: REVELATION 7:9-17

This passage is one that Stephen looks at in the main session, and could be expanded upon in a sermon.

👉 OPTION TWO: ACTS 11:21-26

This is part of the passage the Bible study is based on (see next page), which could also be expanded upon in a sermon.

👉 OPTION THREE: MICAH 6:6-8

This passage is not mentioned in this session, but is a passage that could be used to summarize the whole course, if you have not used it in Session 4:

- How does God want us to live; what pleases him? We have many false answers to this question.
- God says that we must do justice (not just think or talk about it); love mercy (not grudgingly give it); and walk humbly with God.
- This is a living faith: genuine devotion to Christ, but a practical and relational outworking of it in the real world.

If one of your Sunday sermons is to be based on the theme of this session, church members will find a page to write notes on the sermon on page 151 of their Handbooks.

BIBLE STUDY

AIM: The main session showed us the breathtaking vision of God's ultimate plan for the world: the church triumphant—people of all nations united in Christ in the new creation. This Bible study will underline this vision for your group, and help them to see that struggling with racial division and suspicion in the church is nothing new. Under God we must strive to realize this vision in the church militant—our congregational life now.

NOTE: This session roams around the Bible quite a bit, in order to show God's love of diversity in his people. Try not to get bogged down in the detail of each passage, but keep the study moving along. The main passage establishes the principle, and the rest of the study seeks to show how that is played out in the rest of the Bible, and the challenge it brings to us today. Try to spend as much time as you can on the opening question, 4 and 5.

Discuss

The Bible presents us with a breathtaking vision of God's ultimate plan for the world. A new community of God's people from every nation, tribe and level of society, united in Christ forever. But Christians have often struggled to live out the reality of God's global plan in our churches today.

Why do we prefer to spend time with "people like us"? Is that a good or a bad thing?

> Try to broaden this discussion to the widest range of categories possible. It's often true with regard to gender, wealth and social group, as well as our ethnic and language group. Some reasons might include:
>
> - We enjoy spending time with people who are interested in the same things or share a common history.
> - We are easily understood in these groups. People just "get us" without us having to explain things.
> - You can get on with enjoying friendships without barriers.
> - Relationships with "people like us" usually take a lot less time and energy.

- The problem is that groups can easily strengthen and define themselves by putting other groups down along the lines of gender, race, class, etc.

How can this happen in churches? Is that a good or bad thing?

- Churches can easily become monochrome culturally—that may simply reflect the area they are in, or even be due to a deliberate choice in order to reach certain groups effectively, like college students or creatives.
- Even when church members do not have bad attitudes toward other groups, they can easily make people who are "different" in some way feel very uncomfortable about being part of the group.
- At its worst, this tendency will make people feel both excluded and rejected.

 READ ACTS 11:1-18

¹ Now the apostles and the brothers who were throughout Judea heard that the Gentiles also had received the word of God. ² So when Peter went up to Jerusalem, the circumcision party criticized him, saying, ³ "You went to uncircumcised men and ate with them."

This is a report of what happened to Peter when God led him to share the gospel with Cornelius—a God-fearing Gentile, as reported in greater detail in the rest of chapter 11. This is a very big moment in the life of the early church.

1. Why was this event such a big deal for the early church?

This was the first time that a Gentile received the sign of genuine conversion to Christ—the gift of the Holy Spirit. This was an enormous deal for the early church, which was made up almost entirely of Jewish people. Jesus was born a Jew and in his teaching ministry came primarily for "the lost sheep of Israel" (Matthew 15:24). Jewish people felt superior in so many ways to Gentiles—they had the law and the temple, and were the people of God and descendants of Abraham. They were a persecuted and occupied people, which would have stoked their hostility toward outsiders. They simply had no sense that Jesus had come for anyone but the Jewish nation.

It is clear that this was such a big deal because Peter required a lot of convincing. God gave him a vision, repeated three times, where he commanded him to do something that was against his cultural instincts as a Jewish man—eat non-*kosher* food. God gave a clear, unmistakable sign when Cornelius embraced the gospel message that Jesus is Lord—he spoke in tongues in just the same way that the Jewish disciples had when they received the Spirit. It was the final piece of evidence for Peter that God was doing a new thing—bringing salvation to the world.

What hints and indications does the Old Testament give that the gospel is for the whole world? What should Peter, as a Jew, have already known? (See Isaiah 42:5-7; Psalm 67; Acts 1:8; 8:4-8, 27; John 10:16; 12:20-23; Matthew 15:22-28; Jonah.)

- The Old Testament is full of stories of non-Jews being blessed by God. Ask the group to see how many they can name!
- Jesus' teaching also pointed in the same direction. He has "other sheep that are not of this fold"; and he announces that his hour has finally come when Greeks come to seek him.
- Jesus hints at the widening circles of gospel proclamation and response in the commission in Acts 1:8.
- Already, through the ministry of Philip, outsiders were being joined to the church. Samaritans responded to the gospel. They had a tenuous claim to be Jewish, and were reviled by many who thought themselves to be "pure blood." And the Ethiopian eunuch was also converted to Christ.

2. What does the reaction of the "circumcision party" show about their understanding (Acts 11:2-3)?

Instead of rejoicing in the work of God in Cornelius's life, they criticized him for eating with a Gentile. It was very hard for them to accept how radical a change the gospel brought. They were used to thinking they were special—and indeed they were and are. But now that God was dealing with all people in the same way, they were defensive.

How do they respond when they hear the full story (v 17-18)?

- They stop arguing, and praise God.
- They accept that God is doing a new thing, and that his calling of non-Jews is valid.

READ ACTS 11:19-26

> *19 Now those who were scattered because of the persecution that arose over Stephen traveled as far as Phoenicia and Cyprus and Antioch, speaking the word to no one except Jews. 20 But there were some of them, men of Cyprus and Cyrene, who on coming to Antioch spoke to the Hellenists also...*

3. What happened in Antioch that confirmed what started with Cornelius?

- Initially the gospel was only being declared to the Jews by Jesus-following Jews who had come from Jerusalem after Stephen was killed.
- Other Jewish believers in Jesus turned up, however, and began speaking to non-Jews, who embraced Jesus as their Lord enthusiastically.
- The apostles in Jerusalem send Barnabas, who witnesses the revival among Gentiles first hand. He teaches and encourages them.
- He hunts out Paul to help him run this new church.
- People there are first called "Christians."

4. What signs can you think of from the rest of the New Testament that, as the church continued to grow and spread, it was marked by both its enormous diversity and its wonderful unity in Christ?

You might ask the group from their Bible knowledge to name as many different kinds of people as they can who they know were joined together in the early church. There is ample evidence in the rest of the New Testament that the early Christians formed a hugely diverse gathering, not just from different races but from different social groups—rich and poor, young and old, aristocracy, merchants, professionals and farmers, and both male and female. A few examples:
- Acts 16: The first converts in Philippi were a businesswoman (Lydia), a demon-possessed slave girl, and the Philippian jailer (probably a retired soldier) and his family.
- The book of James describes a church life that includes both rich and poor feasting together in the same congregation.
- Young people were clearly part of the congregations, e.g. Eutychus (Acts 20:9), and Timothy, who knew the gospel from his mother and grandmother.
- Paul encourages Philemon and the slave Onesimus to accept one another as part of the body of Christ.

- Many women are mentioned and honored in Paul's letters and in the Gospels. It was reported that many women followed Jesus and supported him, including members of the royal household (Luke 8:2-3).
- Paul's instructions on relationships (e.g. Ephesians 5:22 – 6:5) clearly show that congregations included husbands and wives, children and parents, slaves and masters.
- 1 Corinthians 6:9-11: There was also a diversity in reputation. People who were liars, drunks, sexual perverts, thieves, etc. had become Christians and were now part of the people of God.

How can this rich diversity be such a powerful testimony to the grace of God both then and today?

- It is miraculous. By our nature we tend to stick with people like us. That we are formed into a loving fellowship with others unlike us is nothing short of a miracle of grace.
- It shows that we are different than the world around us. The world will tend to categorize people as us and them. By being united in Christ, we show that God's choice is more important than our own.
- This rich, diverse community is an imperfect picture of God's plan for all eternity in the new creation.
- The presence of saved sinners in our congregation is testimony to the grace of God in forgiving and restoring all kinds of people (see the list in 1 Corinthians 6:9-11).

5. **What signs can you think of in the rest of the New Testament that it remained a struggle to strive for this unity in diversity?**

Encourage the group to come up with ideas from their own Bible knowledge. If there are none forthcoming, give them the Bible passages below to look up.

- Acts 15: Varying traditions between Jewish and Gentile believers were a considerable point of tension in the early church; so much so that they needed a council meeting to decide on the issue. The "Jerusalem statement" affirms the teaching that the cultural differences between the two wings are not fundamental, but pleads for cultural understanding and sensitivity, so that brothers and sisters are not outraged by each other's behavior.

- Paul's "household codes," which appear in several of his letters (e.g. Colossians 3:18 – 4:1), show that Christians needed reminding and teaching about their responsibilities to each other. The implication is that they were failing each other in these regards.
- Galatians 2:11-14: Even Peter failed in this regard—he wanted Gentile Christians to conform to Jewish ways of religious practice. Paul opposed him as he saw that this undermined the gospel message.
- James's teaching about rich and poor (2:1-9) shows that there remained ingrained patterns of behavior among the rich.
- Acts 6:1-7: The Greek widows were getting left out in the provision of food— maybe not deliberately, but it was felt deeply by them. The response was to create a group of workers who were mostly of culturally Greek origin (we can infer this from their names).

Apply

FOR YOUR CHURCH: Where do we feel the same pressures today in our churches? How can you protect yourself from slipping back into worldly ways of thinking in this area?

It would be a mistake to make this question about just your own church, or just about race. Try to encourage your group to think more widely: young v old; poor v rich; men v women. Our acceptance, unity and love for each other should be without question.

The gospel is the answer to this. God has called us to belong to him. Who are we to argue with that? He has made us brothers and sisters in Christ—people we will share eternity with. That is something that should silence our objections and lead us to glorify God—and then to embrace our brothers and sisters, whoever they might be.

IN YOUR COMMUNITY: This miraculous unity in diversity in Christ is something which is a unique gift to the church. But Christians should also be working to establish the equality and validity of every person in society. How does 2 Corinthians 5:14-16 help us see why we should be involved in this wider work?

- *"We regard no one according to the flesh"* (v 16): The world categorizes people in all kinds of ways. We categorize everyone in one way: everyone is a precious human being made in the image of God, and a sinner who needs to know Christ to find forgiveness.

- *"The love of Christ controls us"* (v 14): Jesus death was "for all"—people from every tribe and nation. Our motivation is to win people for Christ, whoever they are.
- Every single human being has a fundamental dignity and worth. Any time that dignity is mocked, excluded or diminished, we should be incensed by it.
- What simple practical things can you do that will encourage the practice of a godly diversity in your church and in society?

FOR YOURSELF: What simple practical things can you do that will encourage the practice of a godly diversity in your church and in society?

Encourage the group to come up with very practical suggestions. For example:
- sit next to someone different than you in church: different ethnicity, age, social class, etc.
- take the initiative to strike up conversations across boundaries.
- survey your friendship group. Is everyone the same general type? Actively pursue difference.
- pray that God would silence your instinctive cultural reactions to people who are different, and that you would praise God for his grace in rescuing all kinds of different people.
- work out ways you can push back in a positive way against the kind of low-level racist or ageist cultural "humor" that is part of many conversations.

Pray

FOR YOURSELF: Pray that you would learn to silence your instinctive reactions to people who are different, and praise God for his love for all people. Pray that you would view all people as precious souls made in the image of God and in need of Christ's forgiveness.

FOR YOUR CHURCH: Pray that your church would become a richly diverse community that delights in God's grace and calling.

FURTHER READING

> When the gospel enables us to live in love, even though we may have nothing else in common save Christ, it is a testimony to its power to transform a group of sinful, self-centered people into a loving community united by a common relationship with Jesus Christ.
> **Mark Dever**

> The bloodline of Jesus Christ is deeper than the bloodlines of race. The death and resurrection of the Son of God for sinners is the only sufficient power to bring the bloodlines of race into the single bloodline of the cross.
> **John Piper**

> If [God] doesn't show partiality, neither should we ... There is richness in knowing—really knowing—someone who is different than you.
> **Trillia J. Newbell**

Books

- Bloodlines: Race, Cross, and the Christian (John Piper)
- Under Our Skin (Benjamin Watson)
- One New Man: The Cross and Racial Reconciliation in Pauline Theology (Jarvis Williams)
- Disunity in Christ: Uncovering the Hidden Forces that Keep Us Apart (Christena Cleveland)
- Strong and Weak (Andy Crouch)

Online

- Don't Like Diversity? You'll Hate Heaven: gospelshapedchurch.org/resources571
- Racial Diversity and Our "Third Race": gospelshapedchurch.org/resources572
- Racial Reconciliation, the Gospel, and the Church: gospelshapedchurch.org/resources573
- Must Every Church Be Multi-Ethnic? (Video) gospelshapedchurch.org/resources574
- Black and White Is Not a Black-and-White Issue: gospelshapedchurch.org/resources575
- Why Racial Reconciliation Is a Gospel Issue: gospelshapedchurch.org/resources576

LEADER'S REFLECTIONS

GOSPEL SHAPED

CHURCH

The Complete Series

LET THE POWER OF THE GOSPEL SHAPE FOUR OTHER CRITICAL AREAS IN THE LIFE OF YOUR CHURCH

"WE WANT CHURCHES CALLED INTO EXISTENCE BY THE GOSPEL TO BE SHAPED BY THE GOSPEL IN THEIR EVERYDAY LIFE."

DON CARSON AND TIM KELLER

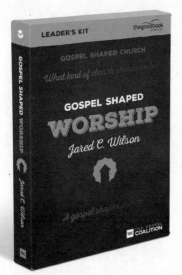

GOSPEL SHAPED
WORSHIP

Christians are people who have discovered that the one true object of our worship is the God who has revealed himself in and through Jesus Christ.

But what exactly is worship? What should we be doing when we meet together for "church" on Sundays? And how does that connect with what we do the rest of the week?

This seven-week whole-church curriculum explores what it means to be a worshiping community. As we search the Scriptures together, we will discover that true worship must encompass the whole of life. This engaging and flexible resource will challenge us to worship God every day of the week, with all our heart, mind, soul and strength.

Written and presented by **JARED C. WILSON**
Jared is Director of Communications at Midwestern Seminary and College in Kansas City, and a prolific author. He is married to Becky and they have two daughters.

WWW.GOSPELSHAPEDCHURCH.ORG/WORSHIP

GOSPEL SHAPED
OUTREACH

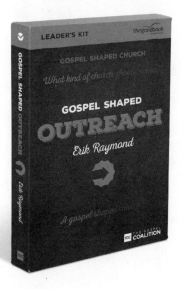

Many Christians are nervous about telling someone else about Jesus. The nine sessions in this curriculum don't offer quick fixes or evangelism "gimmicks." But by continually pointing us back to the gospel, they will give us the proper motivation to work together as a church to share the gospel message with those who are lost without Christ.

As you work through the material, you will discover that God's mission of salvation in the world is also your mission; and that he is inviting you into the privilege of praying and working to advance his kingdom among your family, friends, neighbors, co-workers and community.

Gospel Shaped Church is a curriculum from The Gospel Coalition that will help whole congregations pause and think slowly, carefully and prayerfully about the kind of church they are called to be.

Written and presented by **ERIK RAYMOND**
Erik is the Preaching Pastor at Emmaus Bible Church in Omaha, Nebraska. He is married to Christie and they have six children.

WWW.GOSPELSHAPEDCHURCH.ORG/OUTREACH

"THESE RESOURCES GIVE SPACE TO CONSIDER WHAT A GENUINE EXPRESSION OF A GOSPEL-SHAPED CHURCH LOOKS LIKE FOR YOU IN THE PLACE GOD HAS PUT YOU, AND WITH THE PEOPLE HE HAS GATHERED INTO FELLOWSHIP WITH YOU."

DON CARSON AND TIM KELLER

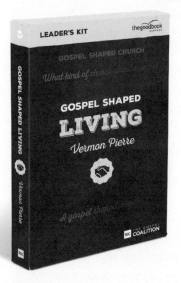

GOSPEL SHAPED
LIVING

Start a fresh discussion in your church about how the gospel of Christ impacts every area of life in our world.

Gospel Shaped Living explores over seven sessions what it means for a local church to be a distinctive, countercultural community.

Through the gospel, God calls people from every nation, race and background to be joined together in a new family that shows his grace and glory. How should our lives as individuals and as a church reflect and model the new life we have found in Christ? And how different should we be from the world around us?

This challenging and interactive course will inspire us to celebrate grace and let the gospel shape our lives day by day.

Written and presented by **VERMON PIERRE**
Vermon is the Lead Pastor of Roosevelt Community Church in Phoenix, Arizona, and a Gospel Coalition council member. He is married to Dennae and they have four children.

WWW.GOSPELSHAPEDCHURCH.ORG/LIVING

GOSPEL SHAPED
WORK

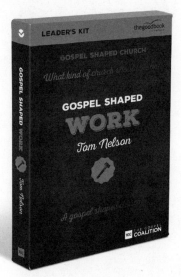

Many Christians experience a troubling disconnect between their everyday work and what they live and work for as a believer in Jesus. How should the gospel shape my view of life on an assembly line, or change my work as a teacher, artist, nurse, home-maker or gardener?

Gospel Shaped Work explores over eight sessions how the gospel changes the way we view our work in the world—and how a church should equip its members to serve God in their everyday vocations, and relate to the wider world of work and culture.

These engaging and practical sessions are designed to reveal the Bible's all-encompassing vision for our daily lives, and our engagement with culture as a redeemed community. They will provoke a fresh discussion in your church about how the gospel of Christ impacts every area of life in our world.

Written and presented by **TOM NELSON**
Tom is the Senior Pastor of Christ Community Church in Kansas City, and president of *Made To Flourish network*. He is married to Liz and they have two grown children.

WWW.GOSPELSHAPEDCHURCH.ORG/WORK

MORE RESOURCES
TO HELP SHAPE YOUR
CHURCH

Let the gospel frame the way you think and feel

This workbook shows how ordinary Christians can live the life that God calls us to. By focusing our attention on the gospel, everyday problems familiar to Christians everywhere can be transformed as the cross of Christ becomes the motive and measure of everything we do. *Gospel Centered Life* shows how every Christian can follow the way of the cross as they embrace the liberating grace of God in Christ.

STEVE TIMMIS is Global Director for Acts 29

TIM CHESTER is a teacher, pastor and author

WWW.THEGOODBOOK.COM/GCL

LIVE**DIFFERENT**

" I HAVE COME THAT THEY MAY HAVE LIFE, AND HAVE IT TO THE FULL. "

━━━ JOHN 10:10 ━━━

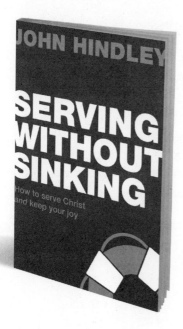

"As I was reading John's book, I found myself in conversations with some of the very people it addresses—people who serve, but who are growing weary of serving. It was a joy to recommend the book to them."

Tim Challies
BLOGGER & AUTHOR

This warm and pastoral book by Tim Lane helps readers to see when godly concern turns into sinful worry, and how Scripture can be used to cast those worries upon the Lord. You will discover how to replace anxiety with peace in your life, freeing you to live life to the full.

TIM LANE is President of the Institute for Pastoral Care, USA, and co-author of *How People Change*

WWW.THEGOODBOOK.COM/LD

the**good**book
COMPANY

LIVE | GROW | KNOW

Live with Christ, Grow in Christ, Know more of Christ.

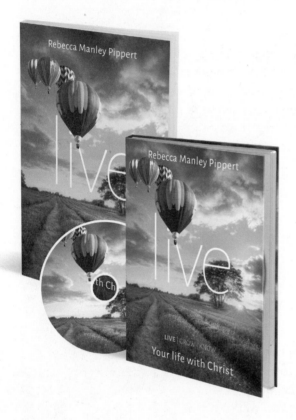

"These studies by Becky Pippert are clear and accessible, yet substantial and thoughtful explorations of how to be grounded and grow in Christian faith. They evidence years of experience working with people at all stages of belief and skepticism. I highly recommend them."

Tim Keller

PART 1
live

Explores what the Christian life is like

Ever got to the end of running an evangelistic course and wondered: What next?

LiveGrowKnow is a brand new series from globally renowned speaker Rebecca Manley Pippert, designed to help people continue their journey from enquirer to disciple to mature believer.

LIVE, consists of five DVD-based sessions and is the perfect follow-up to an evangelistic course or event, or for anyone who wants to explore the Christian life more deeply.

REBECCA MANLEY PIPPERT

Globally renowned speaker and author of
Out of the Saltshaker

PART **2**

grow

Explores how we
mature as Christians

I'm a Christian… what next? The studies in GROW show what God's plan for
our lives is, and how we can get going
and get growing in the Christian life.

KNOW looks at the key doctrines of
the Christian faith, going on a rapid
ride through eternity past, creation,
the fall, redemption and Christ's
future return.

PART **3**

know

Looks at core
doctrines of the faith

EXPLORE
BY THE BOOK

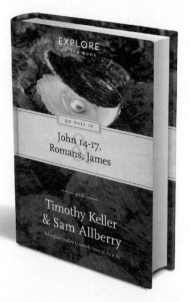

Timothy Keller and Sam Allberry sit alongside you as you open up the treasures of John 14 – 17, Romans and James. These inspirational daily readings, taken from the popular *Explore* Bible devotional, are presented in beautiful hardback format, complete with ribbon marker and space for journaling.

Find strength in God's word each day with the *Explore by the Book* series. These beautiful hardback books contain a mix of our bestselling devotionals from some of our most-loved authors, including Mark Dever, Timothy Keller and Mike McKinley. There are readings for 90 days in each, with space for journaling and a ribbon marker.

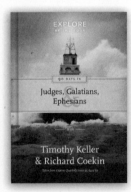

5 THINGS TO PRAY

We all want to pray and know it's important, but we can get stuck in a rut. These books will give you lots of ideas when you don't know what to pray. For each passage of Scripture there are five things to pray.

Wondering what to pray for your church? These fresh ideas will help you pray in line with God's will.

Transform how you pray for your friends and family. Use in your personal devotions or with a friend.

[GOD'S WORD FOR YOU]

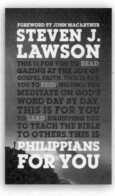
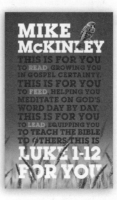
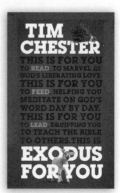

God's Word for You is a series of expository guides which walk you through books of the Bible verse by verse. These flexible resources can be read cover to cover, used for daily devotions, and used to lead small-group Bible studies, or to teach the word of God in your church. See the full range and their associated small-group study guides online.

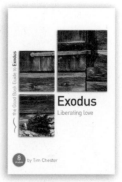